BASIC BOOKS IN EDUCATION

Editor: *Kathleen O'Connor, B.Sc., Senior Lecturer in Education, Rolle College, Exmouth*
Advisory Editor: *D. J. O'Connor, M.A., Ph.D. Professor of Philosophy, University of Exeter*

An Introduction to the Sociology of Education

This book is seen as a foundation for a basic course in the sociology of education. The authors have selected material from the literature of the sociology of education which is of direct relevance and interest to the teacher.

After explaining and defining some basic concepts in sociology, the authors introduce the student to the topic of the family and socialisation leading on to an examination of the sociological aspects of education and the educational system, including teacher-learner relationships, and the class as a group.

Complex issues have been simplified by utilising contemporary sociological models which should help students to organise educational information they will collect during their course.

Key words in the text are in SMALL CAPITALS, there are summaries and 'further reading' lists at the end of each chapter and there is a full bibliography, glossary and index.

An Introduction to the Sociology of Education

BRIAN J. ASHLEY, B.Sc.(Econ.)
PRINCIPAL LECTURER IN SOCIOLOGICAL STUDIES
MORAY HOUSE COLLEGE OF EDUCATION

HARRY COHEN, B.A.
LECTURER IN SOCIOLOGY
MORAY HOUSE COLLEGE OF EDUCATION

ROY G. SLATTER, B.A.
PRINCIPAL LECTURER IN SOCIOLOGY
ELIZABETH GASKELL COLLEGE

MACMILLAN
London . Melbourne . Toronto
1969

Published by
MACMILLAN AND CO LTD
Little Essex Street London WC2
and also at Bombay Calcutta and Madras
Macmillan South Africa (Publishers) Pty Ltd Johannesburg
The Macmillan Company of Australia Pty Ltd Melbourne
The Macmillan Company of Canada Ltd Toronto
Gill and Macmillan Ltd Dublin

Printed in Great Britain by
RICHARD CLAY (THE CHAUCER PRESS) LTD
Bungay, Suffolk

Contents

Preface

We see this book as a foundation for a basic course in the sociology of education for students of education. For this reason, we have tried to avoid the problem of providing a mass of information from sociology which is only broadly relevant to education. Instead, we have tried to provide a consistent framework within which to look at such material. Although the framework adopted for this book is based essentially on the work of Talcott Parsons, we have taken the liberty to modify it to meet our own requirements and to take account of the problem of dealing with change within the system. We emphasise that it is simply an approach among many, but we hope it will familiarise the student with some aspects of current functional theory and how this may be applied to the analysis of educational systems.

Inevitably, we have to select certain material from the considerable body of research findings and literature which is resulting from the interests of sociologists in all educational institutions. We have restricted our concern largely to those areas of the educational process of direct relevance and interest to the teacher. We have also simplified complex issues by constructing models, which we hope will help students to organise information they will collect in the course of their studies.

Our experience with students of education suggests that they have specific needs and that it is important to resist the temptation to teach sociology for its own sake rather than to meet those needs.

We hope, however, that by helping students to understand some relevant problems they may wish to continue to read and study within the literature of sociology, and to explore further the real implications the subject has for education.

Acknowledgements

Our thanks are due to Dr P. Musgrave who originally suggested that we undertake this book and to our colleagues with whom we have discussed a number of issues. The responsibility for the content is, of course, our own.

We are also indebted to Mrs M. Baxter, Mrs D. Clouston and Miss Nancy Watt who typed the script and to our wives for acting as proof-readers.

1 Introduction

EDUCATIONAL SOCIOLOGY AND THE SOCIOLOGY OF EDUCATION

The distinction between educational sociology on the one hand and the sociology of education on the other is one which sociologists have come to emphasise in recent years. It reflects the growing interest which sociologists are taking in all aspects of education. The difference is more than a sterile argument between pedantic academics; it suggests a divergence in perspective and method. However, there is probably an element of gamesmanship involved as implied by Hansen when he considers that at times 'the terms are used in a sort of academic one-upmanship, in which the sociologist may not be attempting to one-up the educator so much as to protect himself from one downery at the hands of his colleagues'.[1]* All new fields of research have to face the problem of obtaining recognition from those which are already established.

The term EDUCATIONAL SOCIOLOGY dates back to the early part of this century when educational sociology was being offered as a subject in a number of colleges and universities in the United States.[2] It had neither developed a sound theoretical framework nor a rigorous methodology but was more of an educational discipline than a sociological one. The educational sociologists attempted to introduce a moral element into the discipline, based on a belief then current that social science could provide the guidelines for the aims and values of education.

The use of the term SOCIOLOGY OF EDUCATION is part of the attempt to throw off this tradition of moral commitment and to bring the discipline into line with the rest of sociology. This involves the study of educational institutions using theoretical

* Small numbers refer to notes at the end of the chapter.

models and methodological techniques developed by sociologists. It is in sharp contrast with the view of the educationalist who is inclined to use sociology wherever it can help him, without paying much attention to rigorous theory and precise methodology. In educational sociology where this was the practice, both the student and the teacher found the approach inadequate as it lacked unity.

In the United States and Britain the term educational sociology has lost ground to the new description of the discipline, the sociology of education. Hansen suggests that the sociologist, by maintaining a dispassionate objectivity, is refraining from social action. The educationalist, on the other hand, must be involved in social action. It appears to us that sociology of education is the bridge between the two. Our role is to interpret the work of the one to the other. Hansen has suggested that the two terms be retained – educational sociology for the pursuit of a normative theory of education and research; and sociology of education for the pursuit of empirical theory and research.[3] This would retain the two separate usages and meanings which have emerged out of the development of the discipline. We need not go as far as Hansen, but certainly the idea of attempting to create a value-free sociology of education is as impossible as a value-free sociology. It is important to retain some of the moral concerns of the educational sociologist and not to limit ourselves to studying only empirical problems, although these are important and essential. We should sometimes concern ourselves with wider issues requiring *value judgements* as to, say, the desirability of one educational system or another, or one ideology or another. A sound modern sociology of education should retain both the empirical and normative element.

A SYSTEMATIC APPROACH TO THE STUDY OF SOCIETY AND EDUCATION

In studying society, most sociologists find it necessary to postulate some type of framework for the analysis and explanation of the data they collect. The view that society can be seen as a SOCIAL SYSTEM is an attempt to give the ever-increasing amount of information some coherence and systemisation. By doing this, sociologists hope to develop a working model at least on the conceptual level of a society, enabling them to classify and possibly explain the information they gather, and obtain an increased understanding of human action.

According to the American sociologist, Talcott Parsons (84),* human action can be classified into four sub-systems which together form a human action system. All human behaviour involves action by some biological being. There is therefore:

1. *The biological system*
   The organic individual develops a personality while inter-acting with other persons in the socio-cultural environment it exists in. We therefore have
2. *The personality system*
   which in interaction with others constitutes
3. *The social system*
   and
4. *The cultural system.*

This process of interaction leads to the social system which Parsons claims is 'analytically independent of both personal and cultural systems'.[4] It is with the social system and to some extent the cultural system that we are concerned in this book.

The use of the word 'system' implies that it is an organised complex whole, which in turn constitutes a set of connected parts. G. C. Homans refers to the philsopher, A. N. Whitehead, as say-ing the concept of an organised whole, or system, existing in an environment is 'a fundamental concept which is essential to scientific theory'.[5] This lends support to the *systematic approach* adopted in this book.

AN OUTLINE OF THE APPROACH IN THIS BOOK
The basis for this book is the increasing need for the educator to understand the society in which the educational system is placed and with which it is engaged in reciprocal interaction. This need for understanding the inseparable nature of the one with the

* Numbers in parentheses refer to Bibliography, pages 141 ff.

other at every level of education is the essence of the sociology of education as explained in the last section.

In applying a systematic approach we have tried to maintain some unity in the manner in which each area of concern is dealt with. As we have emphasised the reciprocal nature of the relation between each system and the wider system, we devote chapter 2, after an outline of basic concepts, to an analysis of the wider social system. To do this we explain briefly and minimally the theory of Talcott Parsons. As in the rest of the book, the analysis is related to education. Lack of space prevents us from providing more than the briefest of sociological perspectives of modern society. The student will, however, be aware of the need to be informed regarding the widest aspects of social life and to be sensitive to the process of social change.

We concentrate upon that aspect of social life which we consider to be the primary process of learning within the wider social system, namely *socialisation*. To do this we need, first of all, to examine the sub-system of society within which socialisation mainly occurs. Therefore, we spend considerable time in describing the family and its relationship to the wider system, as well as the effects of social change upon the family, before discussing the stages of socialisation.

As the student reads through the book it will be apparent that the same framework for analysis is used for each section. One of the major claims of the systematic approach is that the users regard it as being capable of being applied to a whole society or to political, economic or educational organisations and even to small groups such as the family.

Therefore, in chapter 4 when we deal with the sub-system with which we are primarily concerned (namely the educational system), we follow the same procedure as with the family sub-system. Certain aspects of each sub-system, for example, the political or the economic, are not developed as fully as we should like for each could occupy a book in itself, but in each section one of the sub-systems is dealt with in greater detail both as an example of the application of our principles and because we consider it to be a particularly important aspect of the system to the educationalist. We have been careful, however, to document the evidence to which we refer so that the student can expand the content we provide to suit his own purpose.

In our final chapter, we concentrate on the teaching-learning process by dealing with the school as a system and then by analysing the classroom-group itself.

Throughout the book we introduce the student to models which we hope will be applied to and tested against a variety of information and situations beyond these which we are able to mention.

SUMMARY

After discussing the different approaches of educational sociology and the sociology of education, we suggest that the sociologist studying educational institutions, while maintaining his professional objectivity, must become concerned with educational value judgements. In attempting to interpret educational institutions, sociologically, we outline a systematic approach which we use to maintain unity in our material.

NOTES

1. See Hansen, D. A. 'The Uncomfortable Relation of Sociology and Education' in Hansen and Gerstl (41), page 21.
2. Corwin (15), chapter 3.
3. Hansen (41), page 22.
4. Parsons (83), page 7.
5. Homans (46), page 87.

FURTHER READING

Musgrave (78) gives more detailed information in the areas to which we provide an introduction. There are further books of this kind mentioned in the bibliography, i.e. Banks (4) and Corwin (15).

Welford (101) provides the student with a number of useful articles to assist with an understanding of contemporary society seen from the point of view of different specialisms within sociology.

A number of articles are also contained in Hansen (41) which will introduce students to a sociological view of education.

Parsons (83) provides a relatively simple explanation of his theory of the social system and also an example of its application in the analysis of certain societies.

2 Some Basic Concepts

In this chapter we deal with the fundamental concepts which are needed to understand the social system. In doing so we will define these concepts and show how they are inter-related when considered as the essential elements of a social system. We consider it necessary to devote a chapter to discussing basic sociological concepts as students tend to have difficulty with these terms when they first meet them. Many students regard much of the current sociological literature as being unnecessarily weighted with jargon. In many cases this might, in fact, be so, and should be heartily criticised, but the sociologist, in some respects, is justified in attempting to develop a precise terminology. Precision and clarity are necessary in any science and attempts to distinguish between common usage of terms and sociological usage is justified if the common usage is confused. It is not our aim in this book to give final and precise definitions of terms, there are many excellent dictionaries which serve this purpose[1]; instead we attempt to provide the student with 'working' definitions which will allow him to follow what is discussed.

The late C. Wright Mills answering the question of whether we sometimes need technical terms, replied

Of course we do, but 'technical' does not necessarily mean difficult, and certainly it does not mean jargon. If such technical terms are really necessary and also clear and precise, it is not difficult to use them in a context of plain English and thus introduce them meaningfully to the reader.[2]

This is the approach we will try to adopt. The student who feels a need for greater precision should follow up the further reading for this section.

Although other concepts will be introduced and defined the

following are the central concepts discussed in this chapter; interaction, norms, roles and status, groups, and the social system. We deal with each in turn and link them to each other in the social system.

INTERACTION AS THE BASIC PROCESS

Social action

In order to understand what we mean by social interaction, it is necessary to examine the concept of social action. This concept forms the basis of the theories of the German sociologist, Max Weber. He believed that action was non-social when 'oriented solely to the behaviour of inanimate objects'.[3] He regards, for example, a collision of two cyclists as a natural event. It is only when the cyclists take steps to avoid each other, both possibly turning in the same direction, and thus colliding, that we have a social act. In other words, when the two cyclists take account of each others' likely actions and consider the possible effects of their own actions, we have social action taking place.

Weber constructed a typology of social action consisting of four basic types. Social acts are obviously not all the same and it would be useful to be able to categorise social action. He did this as follows:

1. Rational social action in which the actor chooses, purposefully, the most appropriate means for the successful attainment of his rational ends. Weber regarded this as the most important type for an understanding of modern society, as much economic activity is of this sort. (*Zweckrational* in German)
2. Rational social action in which the actor chooses appropriate means for the successful attainment of non-rational ends. These ends are regarded as absolute and are beyond question. They involve value judgements which might be culturally determined, such as religious actions. (*Wertrational*)
3. Affectual social action. This means that the action is determined by the emotions or feelings of the actor.
4. Traditional social action. This is action which is governed by habit and custom. (Traditional)[4]

Throughout his writings Weber makes use of these four types of social action. He shows that most of the actions of people can be analysed using this and similar typologies and that in doing so we can obtain a clearer understanding of our behaviour.

Whatever the type of social action taking place, if the actors are, in fact, considering each others' behaviour and taking account of each other there is social interaction taking place.

Interaction

We may say that the concept of interaction concerns the process which constitutes the very core of social life. It is one of the basic tenets of sociology that the behaviour of human beings can never be fully understood if we do not realise that the social actions of individuals are always oriented towards other human beings. Therefore, the most elementary unit of sociological analysis, unlike psychology, which can study the actions of the individual in isolation, is two individuals mutually influencing each other. We call this process SOCIAL INTERACTION. It may be defined as people mutually and reciprocally influencing each others' expectations of behaviour and actual behaviour. Social interaction occurs when two or more people take account of each other and modify their behaviour; accordingly, Harry M. Johnson, an American sociologist, considers that two persons are interacting when

... each takes account of the other, not merely as a physical object, but as an individual with attitudes, expectations, and the capacity to pass judgement; the action of each is based, to some extent, on his attitudes towards the other and his expectations about the other's probable reactions to him.[5]

This aspect of the actions of one actor setting off a response in the other is quite important and we see interaction taking place as an on-going process, with actions being a stimulus and a response at the same time. Thus interaction is something which is dynamic and not static. It is a continuous process of adjustment and re-adjustment.

There are many different forms of social interaction which we can classify in three broad categories – *co-operation*, *competition* and *conflict*. In actual fact, we could reduce these to two types by saying simply – men can act with each other and against each other. Any society will have social interaction of both types taking place. It would be difficult to say whether the one type is more important than the other. Some sociologists have made more detailed classifications of social interaction including any type of interaction which is essentially *dissociative* or *disjunctive* in the one, and anything which is *associative* or *conjunctive* in the other. Thus, for example, if we were to go into minute detail, interaction would be regarded as dissociative if it were of the following types: disparaging; depreciative; rebuffing or harassing. On the other hand, we would regard interaction as being of the associative type if it was assisting, helping, attracting or aiding some one or a group. These are only some of the possible sub-types of interaction that could be classified. The problem is to develop a classification system which is not too broad a generalisation on the one hand nor too narrow in scope on the other. We must also take care to avoid regarding one form of interaction as being 'better' than the other. Both types are necessary in society.

People interacting are likely to fall into the one form of interaction or another; the degree of consistency in their behaviour is important. It is important for the people concerned and for us trying to understand their behaviour. A person in a given social situation is likely to behave in a co-operative or a competitive manner, depending upon what is expected or required of him in that social situation. An actor comes to learn that in a co-operative situation there are certain required standards of behaviour, just as there are in a competitive situation or any other form of inter-action. We call these standards of behaviour NORMS.

Norms

Most sociologists would probably agree that a norm could be defined as a rule, standard or expected pattern for social action. L. Broom and P. Selznick, in their textbook on sociology, put it in the following way: '. . . norms are blueprints for behaviour, setting limits within which individuals may seek alternate ways to achieve their goals'.[6]

Notice that a norm is not a statistical average, it is a cultural definition of what people consider to be desirable behaviour. By desirable, we are suggesting that norms refer to what ought to be, not what is.

Some sociologists consider that the possession of norms is the

B

distinguishing feature between human societies and animal societies. Kingsley Davis (19), in particular, makes this distinction when he discusses what he calls *the double reality*. That is, the existence of a normative order and a factual order. He says an important point to consider is that norms are not 'real things', something we can see. They are ideas which people have about how others, and they themselves, ought to behave. Norms are not the actual actions of the people interacting. They are, therefore, part of the subjective world of the actor.

There are numerous ways of classifying norms. One of the most commonly used is in terms of the strength of the sanctions if the norms are broken, or rewards if kept. For example, MORES (singular MOS) are norms which, if broken, are punishable by extreme forms of sanctions, usually death or banishment. On the other hand, FOLKWAYS are punishable by far less stringent sanctions. Folkways are usually enforced by such measures as gossip, ridicule and sometimes ostracism.

Folkways are probably familiar to most classroom teachers, as the norms controlling much of the pupils' classroom behaviour are of this type.

Another method of classifying norms is to distinguish between those which are enforced *formally* – that is, when a specific body is set up to determine and administer the sanction – and those which are enforced *informally*. In this case the sanctions are determined and administered by the group of people most directly concerned with the norm, e.g. the family or friends. This would distinguish, on the one hand, between mores and folkways, which are informally enforced, and customary law and enacted law on the other, which are formally enforced by the police and law courts. In our society, the more important mores and folkways have become law; nevertheless, there are still mores in certain groups, which, if broken, carry extreme sanctions. It is not unheard of for a criminal group to injure severely or kill a member who breaks a basic mos. This would be an extreme sanction administered informally or outside the formal system. Other folkways which suffer relatively mild sanctions and are informally enforced are fashion, fad, convention and etiquette.

Norms may be either prescriptive or proscriptive. A *prescriptive norm* is one which indicates to the actor what he should do or how he ought to conduct himself. A *proscriptive norm* indicates to the actor what he should not do or what he ought to avoid doing. During the day to day activities of people, norms are being prescribed and proscribed for them in their interaction with others. This process begins in the family, during the early socialisation of the child, and is continued in school and later at work. The child's own pattern of behaviour is 'controlled' by the norms of the groups of people surrounding him. The fact that the family, wider group or community hold the norms, to some extent gives the norm authority over the individual.

Blake and Davis, in an article on norms and values, remark that the dividing line between the two concepts is always 'fuzzy' and that the attempt to separate the two concepts is made again and again.[7] A possible solution lies in their suggestion that we could make more satisfactory use of the concept 'value' if we recognised it as a mental construct, which we create for the purpose of analysis and do not regard it as a cause of behaviour. The tendency to use 'values' as an explanation of why people behave in the way they do is not fruitful. A more effective way may be to regard them as 'guide-lines' for behaviour in much the same way as norms are 'blue prints'. A VALUE may be defined as a 'generalised end that guides behaviour towards uniformity in a variety of situations . . .'.[8] There is a suggestion that underlying a number of different norms there might be a more generalised common category, a value. Some examples as defined in this sense would be honesty, loyalty and conscientiousness. In each case the value, such as honesty, refers to a quality in the norm which could be found in many different situations. In a sense, a value is one step further removed from the actual interaction taking place than a norm, this tends to make it a difficult and abstract concept to handle.

Up to this point we have discussed people interacting with each other, taking account of certain norms and values. We may say that a person in this situation is playing a role in accordance with the requirements of the others in the situation. This leads us to our next series of important concepts in the social system. We will discuss these under the general heading of roles.

Roles

Although there is probably a high degree of agreement among sociologists on the importance of the concept of role and related concepts, there is also confusion (7).

We will avoid becoming involved in a verbal discussion on what the definition of a role, position or status should be, and instead simply use certain definitions we regard as the best for our purpose, in writing this book. The student, we hope, will develop to a point where he sees problems in these definitions and goes beyond this introduction to examine inconsistencies. We will take up a position similar to that of Gross, Mason and McEarchen in their study of the role of the school superintendent. [9]

The student will have noticed that much of what we have said so far relies on the concept of expectations. In that social action, interaction and norms are concepts which are defined in terms of people holding expectations about other people. We may briefly define EXPECTATIONS as that part of a person's behaviour which is taking account of the likely future actions of others. In a similar manner as the concepts above, we can define a role of a person in terms of expectations. Before we do so, it might be wise to say what we mean when we use the term SOCIAL POSITION, which is the location of a person in a social system. In any group, organisation or society, people occupy positions relative to other persons. This means that a person, say a student, occupies positions in the college he attends, in the family, the community he belongs to and, of course, in the society as a whole. For example, a young boy might occupy the positions of son, pupil, football player in the local team and youth-club member.

Related to these positions there are other positions filled by incumbents which, taken together, form the organisation or society. In the case of the student teacher there would be other students, lecturers, principals, practising teachers and so on. Each of these positions has a related role. We say that a ROLE is a set of expectations applied to an incumbent in a particular position in the social system. Thus, the student teacher occupies a particular position in the college and, as such, he has a certain role which is defined by the expectations of others. They, too, have positions and hence roles related to the one he is in.

The role simply states the expectations applied to a particular position, unlike the expectations which define a norm. In the case of a norm there is a *definite injuctive element*; that is, an authoritative appeal to the incumbent that he ought to behave in a particular way.

A term which is often used interchangeably with position is STATUS. We consider that, in this case, it would be wise to keep closer to the common-language meaning of the word and regard it as the prestige, power or wealth associated with a particular position. We hold this view simply because it seems that an incumbent's position in society may remain unchanged and yet, his status might be altered. Nevertheless, there is a close tie between a person's status and his position. If status is high, usually the position is important. But it is conceivable that in a socialist revolution, for example, a worker's position might remain the same, but his status could rise. There are other usages of these terms: Kingsley Davis regards the role as being the dynamic aspect of status. Status is seen as being similar to position as discussed above, and role is seen as the actual behaviour of the person occupying the status. In our usage, we will refer to the actual behaviour of the person or actor in a particular position as his ROLE PERFORMANCE. This has sometimes been called 'role enactment' or 'role behaviour' or simply 'a person's role'.

The most important determinants of a person's status and role are his age, sex, race, family and SOCIAL CLASS. In all of them, it is a matter of how these foregoing factors are valued in the total society. Thus, if women or a particular racial group occupy menial positions in a society, this is likely to affect their roles and status in that society. In the same way, the position a person's family occupies in the society will determine, to a large extent, his role and status. The determinants of a person's role and status are usually broken down into two broad types. On the one hand, we have those which are ascribed and, on the other, those which are achieved. When the position is one of ASCRIPTION, then the determinants of the individual's status and role are beyond the control of the individual – such as age, sex, caste and class, which are factors determined by birth. Whereas in a position of

ACHIEVEMENT the determinants of the individual's status and role are, in the main, dependent upon his capacities, abilities and the amount of effort that he has put into his actions. He might become the world heavy-weight boxing champion, the Prime Minister or a teacher and so on, and to some extent this is dependent upon himself. In a feudal or a caste-based society, the ascribed position and resulting status and role of an individual are determined by birth. In South Africa or the USA, a man is born into a position in the society which is racially determined, and his resulting status and role are dependent upon whether he happens to be black or white.

Modern societies tend towards the determining factors being achieved rather than ascribed. Obviously, achieved positions are limited by ascribed positions, with the result that not all positions in the society are open to all members and frequently so-called achieved positions are occupied by persons on the basis of ascription rather than achievement. Theoretically, anyone who is a citizen of a country can become the Prime Minister or President, but in most countries it is highly unlikely that a working-class person will attain that position. We might say that, although theoretically in our society most positions are open to achievement, a person's ascribed position will set limits on his possible achievements.

As we have said, people occupy more than one position each, that is they are members of several different groups and organisations. The result is that they perform multiple roles. This is simply a collection of different roles a person may play as a result of being a member of a number of different systems. In this situation it is highly likely that the actor will find that he is involved in ROLE CONFLICT, that is, that the performance of one role conflicts with the performance of another. For example, a student wishing to demonstrate his political awareness and participation in a radical student association may find that his role performance, in this respect, is in conflict with his role as a 'conscientious student'. This situation, if unresolved, leads to inconsistencies in his behaviour and increased role conflict. This mode of analysis can be applied to all situations, and would be particularly helpful in the classroom, where the role performance of the pupil might conflict with his role performance as a member of a particular group. Thus, the pupil in his role is expected to stay at home and work, but in his role as a member of a friendship group, he is expected to go out with his friends and ignore his school commitments.

In most instances, role conflict is resolved by reference to some sort of scale of priorities. These priorities would be ranked in terms of the values and norms which predominate in the system. These would, in fact, indicate to the actor that the obligations and duties in one role supercede those in another. Thus, in the example of the student discussed above, values of loyalty to his parents and conscientiousness in his work are supporting the one role, and values of freedom, democracy and liberty the other. In cases like this, the conflict remains unresolved as the issues relate to the whole system and to resolve them would imply changing the society, although some might attempt this.

If we examine any particular position, we see that it has its own distinctive role and status, and that every position in society involves not only a single connected role, but a number of connected roles. A teacher, for example, has a particular position, role and status, but there are a number of other positions, roles and statuses specifically related to that of teacher. These are the pupils, headmaster, his colleagues, the educational board, teachers' associations, parents, and any other organisation or person taking a special interest in the teacher's role performance. The existence of this structure of positions related to a specific position could be called a *positional set*. In exactly the same way, we have what we call a ROLE SET and a *status set*. We can easily distinguish between these different types of sets if we recall that the position refers to location, the role to expectations and status to prestige. Role set is the only concept of the three which has been developed. Robert K. Merton defines a role set as ' . . . the complement of role relationships which persons have by virtue of occupying a particular status'.[10] (We would use the word 'position' rather than 'status' in the definition.) It is important to note the difference between 'multiple roles' and 'role sets'. The former refers to a complex of roles associated with a number of positions, whereas the latter refers to a complex of roles associated with one position of the actor or *ego*. Each person in society plays many roles, teacher, father, citizen and so on, these are multiple roles, but each of these roles has a complex of roles associated with it, as pointed out above in the case of a teacher. This complex of roles is the role set. Attached to each role are a number of rights and duties. The role, therefore, has certain obligations which are held as part of the expectations of ego's role set. The people who make up ego's role set may or may not agree on what ego's role obligations are, due in part to demands made on them by the performance of their own roles. INSTITUTIONALISATION of the norms might ensure some agreement concerning the fundamental area of the role, but this agreement can never be perfect. This creates conflict and instability in the role set and can make ego's performance of his role very difficult or very interesting depending upon his perspective. It is important to distinguish the difference between role conflict and this structural instability in the role set. In role conflict there is a conflict in ego as a result of the position he occupies in different systems. The conflict in his role set concerns only one position he occupies and the position occupied by others. The conflict, in this case is built into the system, so to speak, and, as such, is part of the structure of the society or group or system we are dealing with. Merton describes this conflict in a school situation. He says the fact that the members of the school board are often in a social and economic strata quite different from that of the school teacher will mean that, in certain respects, their values and expectations differ from those of the teacher.[11] The teacher may find that the conflict in his role set could include not only the board but also his colleagues, the pupils and parents. Merton suggests that what is regarded as an 'educational frill' by one, might be regarded as being 'essential to education' by someone else. This is obvious in the case of teachers, but it applies to all positions in the society and, just as there must be a degree of consensus concerning expectations, so there will inevitably be a degree of conflict. In the case of the teacher, it would be a helpful exercise to work out the likely role set of the pupil and how this influences his classroom behaviour. One of the predominant features in the pupil's role set will be other pupils, who are usually members of a group.

THE IMPORTANCE OF SOCIAL GROUPS

The group

The importance of groups in sociology cannot be over-estimated and some sociologists have gone as far as to define sociology as '. . . the science that deals with social groups'.[12] This is Johnson's view. He elaborates on this by pointing out the obvious value of the study of groups, since we are all born into family groups and most of our life is spent in contact with groups in one way or another. Therefore, any study of social groups will contribute to our self-knowledge. This is all the more valuable for those people who actually work with groups, such as a classroom teacher. In his discussion of groups, Johnson goes on to say: 'Sociology is concerned with interaction itself. A social group is a system of social interaction.'[13]

Thus we can see the link between groups and the process of interaction which we have been discussing. A group may be considered as a system of interaction, which means that a number of people who are interacting with each other can form a group. The term 'group' may be adequate for everyday usage, but we need to state it in more precise terminology. We may say that a SOCIAL GROUP consists of two or more persons who take each other into account in their actions and are, as a result, held together and set apart from others. In other words, a group consists of actors between whom there is ascertainable interaction, and who are bound together and separated from other actors. Not all people who are interacting form a social group. A salesman and his customer are interacting, but do not form a group. In a similar manner, nor do all clusters of people who are physically separated from others form a social group. For example a group of people at a bus queue are held together and separated from others, but do not form a social group. They are simply an aggregate of people. We sometimes group people together in a social class or in the same sex or age category. These are not social groups, but logical ones without any necessary interaction taking place between the members. It is important for the student to think of the social group as a sociological entity and not a mere abstraction. It is of very little value in trying to understand group behaviour if we persist in thinking that the group is a collection of individuals and not something which by interaction and the development of norms is welded into a single entity, and which can be the single most important factor in understanding or explaining a member's behaviour. A group develops characteristics of its own which cannot be understood in terms of the individual members alone. From the teacher's point of view, this means regarding the class as consisting of groups of children and not a collection of individuals.

Primary groups and secondary groups

It is obvious, if we observe groups for any length of time, that there are many different sorts, ranging from the family group to the large bureaucratic organisation. Sociologists have worked out a number of classifications of the different types that can be found. We will discuss some of these.

The most common distinction is that between the primary groups and the secondary groups. Charles Horton Cooley, an American sociologist, was the first to use the concept at the start of this century. In his view, a primary group was characterised by 'intimate face-to-face association of lasting duration, a small number of participants, and a common bond between the members best expressed by a sense of mutual identification.' That is, it created a sense of the 'we' rather than the 'I'. Cooley regarded the groups as being primary mainly because they were 'fundamental in forming the social nature and ideals of the individual'.[14]

A secondary group, in contrast, is large in size and characterised by a lack of intimacy between the participants. There need not be face-to-face association between the members. Whereas in the primary group the relations between the members tend to be emotional, in a secondary group they tend to be cool and impersonal, and far more rationally oriented. Ideal examples of a primary group would be a family, friendship group, or gang; whereas a secondary group would be more like a large Civil Service department, an army, a large industrial firm and a large secondary school.

There have been a number of developments of Cooley's

distinction. A particularly good extension of his ideas is to be found in Kingsley Davis' discussion of the relational aspects of a primary group.[15] There are many similarities between Cooley's distinction and those made by other sociologists, such as, Tonnies' GEMEINSCHAFT and GESELLSCHAFT type societies, Redfield's *folk* and *urban continuum* and Beckers' *sacred* and *secular* distinctions. Although the referents are not the same, the differences tend to be in the same direction. Thus, a folk society would contain virtually only primary groups and an urban society would have many secondary groups.

Our society contains an increasing number of secondary groups. Thus, many writers think that the qualities that emerge out of primary type relationships are endangered. The society, it is argued, is becoming more and more impersonal and BUREAU-CRATIC and, as such, is threatening many of the characteristics associated with the warm and friendly atmosphere of the folk, rural or *gemeinschaft* type life. It is important to note that the primary and secondary groups can both have effects which are commonly regarded as negative or positive. These depend, to a large extent, on how the groups are used and on the observer's values.

The primary group is often regarded as serving a mediating function between the individual and the secondary group. The family, for example, protects its members, as far as it can, from the secondary groups in the wider society. Membership of the primary group provides us with effective emotional satisfaction. It is in the family, a primary group, that people experience deep emotional gratification. On the other hand, it is also in the family that many unsatisfactory emotional experiences occur. A person obtains a sense of identity by being a member of a primary group. This can also be obtained, at least to some extent, in the secondary group, in the form of loyalty to the party or nation. The major DYSFUNCTION of the primary group would be over-integration of the individual, so that he finds difficulty in forming any attachment outside of it.

There are numbers of other classifications, such as IN-GROUP and OUT-GROUP. These terms were used some time ago by Sumner. An in-group is any group which separates itself from other groups and considers itself distinct from these groups. The out-groups are all the groups other than the one considered by the members as distinct. A classification which has been used in much research into group behaviour is that of the formal and informal group (46).

The FORMAL GROUP is one in which the rules governing the interaction are laid down explicitly, each person's role is clearly determined for him, and the positions in the group form a hierarchy strictly related to the rules. The army or the school are good examples; also, most factories have clearly defined formal structures. INFORMAL GROUPS do not have clearly defined rules in that they are not explicitly stated. There is a higher degree of casualness in each person's role. Homans describes in his book, *The Human Group*, an example of an informal group emerging within the formal group of a factory. The informal group has great influence on the productive capacity of the workers. In the same way, informal groups will emerge in the school classroom, which might or might not increase the effectiveness of the teacher. This aspect of group behaviour in the classroom will be discussed in a later chapter.

We can get some idea of the influence the group has over individual behaviour and judgement if we look at two studies by social psychologists.

In the first study, by Muzafer Sherif, use was made of the autokinetic effect in an attempt to demonstrate the relationship between the individual's and the group's norm. The autokinetic effect is the apparent movement of a pin-point of light when viewed in a completely darkened room. This is an ambiguous situation as the light only *appears* to move. Each subject is placed in the room and develops an average assessment. If the individuals are placed in the room in groups of two or three members, 'their judgements converge in a group or standard norm'. Once the individual acquires a group standard, it tends to persist and he does not revert back to his original range.[16] These findings have been confirmed by other experiments.

In another classical study, conducted by Asch, the effects of group pressure on judgements were measured. In this experiment, the subject looked at a card containing a standard line which he had to match with one of three lines on another card. The problem was a simple visual one as the matching line was quite easy to select. Thus, in this case, we have an unambiguous situation which the subject is required to judge. The experimenter had previously instructed a group of persons to give a deliberately incorrect response, thus when the 'naïve' subject came into the room he was placed in a position of 'a minority of one in the midst of a unanimous majority . . .'. The experimenter found that one third of the estimates of the naïve subjects had yielded to the errors suggested by the group.[17] Although the majority of the estimates of the naïve subjects were correct the findings remain significant, particularly when we recall that this was, in fact, an experimental group and not a group in the sense that we have been discussing it. It gives us some idea of how powerful an influence a primary group or friendship group must have on the formation of norms and values held by individual members. The importance of the group's influence on the individual is also seen in Bernstein's work, investigating the effect of social class and primary groups, i.e. the family, on the use of language (see chapter 5).

Reference groups

The concept of reference groups has arisen out of the fact that any person is influenced in the way he behaves, not only by the groups he might be part of, but also by groups he might not be part of. There are two main approaches to reference group theory. The one put forward by Hyman in 1942, is that a reference group is a group with which one compares oneself when making a self-judgement. And the other view, put forward by Sherif and Newcomb, which sees the reference group as a source of the individual's values. This difference is not insurmountable, and it would seem to be possible to link the two views by saying that ego can relate himself to other groups and, in some cases, adopt the values of that reference group and, in others, reject them. Merton, in fact, has put it in the following way:

In general, then, reference-group theory aims to systemise the determinants and consequences of those processes of evaluation and self-appraisal in which the individual takes the values or standards of other individuals and groups as a comparative frame of reference.[18]

If we add that in this process the individual forms his values, we have the two views coming together.

An important point which requires clarification is that in some respects the term 'reference group' is a misnomer, as the term is not only applied to groups, but also to social categories. For example, if you are a soldier your reference group might well be all civilians. However, the term has now gained acceptance; but it is important to remember that the stress is on the reference part and not on the group: the element of referring is the important one. A distinction also needs to be made between a person's reference group and his *membership group*. They can be one and the same thing, but they need not be. A teacher may have all headmasters as a reference group or he may be less ambitious and have other teachers as his reference group. This is particularly so when the reference group is, in fact, a category or a class of people. Quite often people are torn between demands made on them by their membership group, in the form of certain role expectations, and those of the reference group they relate themselves to. An example would be a teacher trained as a professional in his subject and holding his academic association as his reference group, having to compromise his ideals with the realities of his role as a teacher.

We may infer from the attempt to set up a General Teaching Council in Scotland that a large number of teachers hold as their reference groups professions with established councils. (The British Medical Association is seen by many as the ideal example of a professional society – which maintains standards and protects its members.) The teachers who refuse to join the Council and face the possibility of dismissal probably form two groups. Those who regard the powers of the Council as being insufficient when compared to their reference group (the BMA) and those who hold as a reference group abstract ideals, such as freedom. This latter group might see the Council as curtailing the teacher's rights.

Relative deprivation

This was a concept used by Stouffer in his famous study of the American soldier. He found that soldiers tend to refer themselves to other groups, and measure their own status in terms relative to these others. This concept was later developed by Merton and linked with the theory of reference group behaviour. People are inclined to think of themselves as being relatively deprived by comparing their own situation with that of others. Stouffer suggested that relative deprivation was similar to such accepted concepts in sociology as a 'social frame of reference' and 'patterns of expectations'. This allows us to link it with reference group theory.

Merton lists the studies using the concept of relative deprivation in Stouffer's work and discusses them. For example, the married man in the army compares himself to unmarried soldiers and civilians. The married soldier felt that his induction demanded greater sacrifices than the unmarried soldier and civilians. He therefore felt deprived in relation to them.

Merton notes that the negro soldier in the southern states of the USA 'had a position of . . . wealth and dignity when compared with most negro civilians.'[19]

The concept of relative deprivation could be useful in an analysis of the differences between graduate and non-graduate teachers. The non-graduate teacher, in many instances performing the same job, is paid less then the graduate. The non-graduate might, therefore, feel relatively deprived. Much staff-room behaviour and the complex attitudes of professional associations towards each other might be explained in this way.

THE SOCIAL SYSTEM

In the first chapter we outlined certain aspects of what Parsons called 'the human action system'. In this section we are going to continue that discussion, paying particular attention to the social system.

If we consider a situation in which people act with reference to one another, that is, where there is interaction taking place, we will notice that some patterns of interaction tend to be repeated and that most of the people in interacting situations share common definitions of these situations. They know what to expect from one another and the common standards they share we call values and norms. Each person occupies a position or positions in relation to other persons and performs the relevant roles as expected by the others. The regular patterns of interaction can be regarded as institutionalised patterns, and, as such, they have a high degree of stability. The system, therefore, is regarded as being in a state of balance or *equilibrium*, but this is an unreal picture, as systems are continually undergoing change.

We therefore need to examine the system when it is in *disequilibrium* and is changing. We noted in the discussion of position and roles that a system can contain structural factors which introduce conflict. An actor can find, as a result of occupying more than one position, that he is experiencing role conflict between different positions, so located in the social structure that they are incompatible and cannot be maintained at the same time. This can lead to action on the part of the actor designed to change his role himself, or the structure of the system. In the same way, an actor can find that he is in conflict with the members of his role set who define his role in a manner incompatible with the manner in which he defines it. The actor can attempt to influence the role set and change their definition of the situation or change the structure. But these are not the only sources of change in a social system. Change can be introduced due to contact with other systems. Thus, many African societies have undergone radical change due to contact with Western societies. The development of minor systems with different standards and values from the major system can also introduce change. Thus, for example, we could view a social class or status group at times as a system, particularly when it manifests a sense of community or interest. In this case they would share standards and values which might be different from other sub-systems. Conflict would ensue, possibly leading to change in the total system.

This raises a number of problems concerning consensus and conflict which we will return to towards the end of this section.

A model of the social system

The view that society may be seen as a system of inter-related parts is often referred to as a *Holistic* theory. If we consider society as a 'whole', we note that we tend to call something a 'whole' when we can separate or differentiate it from the rest of its environment. In other words, we talk about some things being internal to it, and other things being external. It would, therefore, be useful to analyse a society, or any system which we regard as a 'whole', in terms of those aspects which are either internal or external to it. An analysis needs to go further than locating the object being analysed spatially, particularly if what we are studying is a society in which people are interacting. Therefore, this being a system in which interaction takes place, what people do and the way in which they behave is important. Parsons, in his discussion of the social system, uses two more analytical concepts when looking at how the system functions. These are the MEANS of action on the one hand, and the ENDS to which the action is oriented on the other. People interacting are always doing something towards goals or ends within a certain situation. This situation consists of aspects over which they may have no control, which we call the conditions, and other aspects which they do control, which we call the means they use.

Therefore, if we analyse a system using these four aspects, we arrive at the following model.[20]

	Instrumental (means)	Consummatory (ends)
External	Adaptive Function A	Goal – Attainment Function G
Internal	Pattern-Maintenance and Tension-Management Function L	Integrative Function I

Figure 1   The Social System.

The distinction between *instrumental* and *consummatory* is analogous to the distinction between means and ends. Each cell

C

(LIGA) represents one of the major sub-systems of the total social system. These component parts (sub-systems) of a social system are inter-related and inter-dependent; changes in one part will affect other parts. We will discuss each of the four functional sub-systems in turn, relating them to the whole social system.

1. In cell 'L' Parsons would include the part of the social system which is predominantly concerned with pattern maintenance and control. This would include activities which are mainly 'cultural', such as those found in the following groups: churches, kinship and artistic, and research institutes, universities and schools. In fact, all activities which are primarily educational. Thus the process of socialisation and learning in general would be the major function of this functional sub-system.

2. In cell 'I' Parsons places that part of the social system mainly concerned with the internal integration of the system. All action which is concerned with maintaining the collective element or the communal element in the society would fall into this category. These are functions in the society which serve to maintain the solidarity of the members in it. For instance, any aspects of political behaviour, which are aimed at obtaining agreement to the system. A good example is provided by some nationalist parties, which try to unite people in a common system and attempt to over-ride dividing features, like class. We also include in this cell law courts, which institutionalise the norms of the society, and hospitals and social welfare agencies, which serve to re-integrate certain members back into accepted roles in the society.

Many writers have criticised Parsons on this point, claiming that it is tantamount to saying that anyone who does not accept the standards or roles of the system is deviant, and that this view places undue emphasis on the integrative functions in society. We can see what is meant by this criticism if we look at the case of a nationalist party, which although serving to unite some people in a common bond, also cuts them off from others. Thus, a nationalistic party, or any uniting force, tends at the same time to have a disintegrating effect. Therefore, to suggest that an integrative function is the primary element in a social system is to fail to see the other side of the equation, which is the disintegrative function of the same action.

3. In cell 'G' we have the part of the social system which is, in the main, concerned with the attainment of goals in relation to the external factors in the system's environment. Most political activity would fall here, including some aspects of religion. Both political and religious organisations establish goals for people in society. As in the previous function, when we suggested that integration implies disintegration, one set of goals implies an alternative set. Thus, we would be inclined to regard people who are interacting as forming a system insofar as they accept the same goals. This would raise a number of problems, one of which is – could we, in fact, regard any modern society as forming a system? In many respects this question reflects the use to which this model has been put; although it was primarily designed for studying societies, much of its fruitful work has been on small-scale systems. In relatively small systems (like a factory, school, hospital or prison) goals are clearly and explicitly stated, and there is at least some acceptance of the goals. In other words, they can be clearly seen as a system and, therefore, can readily be analysed using this model.

4. Finally, in cell 'A' we have activity which is more generally adaptive to the wider conditions of the external environment. Included in this sub-system are all functions which are primarily economic. In action of this sort, people are seen as a means to an end. For example, a worker is viewed as an instrument of production, a means towards an economic end, the company's profit. Again, we should note that not all action is adaptive and sometimes the actions of people fail to adapt to the situation. Many problems are raised by this view. For example could we regard non-adaptive behaviour as functional, for the system? This is a difficult question. Some sociologists have tried to show that disintegration or conflict can, in fact, have functional consequences for the system (16). In the same way we could suggest that non-adaptive behaviour could be seen to be functional for the system. In some respects, juvenile delinquency (which, in terms of the systems values, is considered non-adaptive) nevertheless

performs the function of bringing certain problems – e.g. housing, over-crowding and lack of recreation facilities – to the system's notice.

Viewing society as a system has many advantages, the most important of which is that it allows us to discuss human action within a framework. Using this framework, we can then compare one system of interaction with another and possibly gain insights which we might not have arrived at otherwise. It need not be a social system: we could study the educational system and break it down into its four functional sub-systems. We could note the everyday educational actions people are involved in – behaviour of various kinds, going to school or college, learning, writing, taking examinations, being punished, building schools and so on – and attempt to see how these actions fit into the educational system as a whole. That is, by postulating the existence of an educational system in which many of the participants share the same values and norms, we could possibly understand the ordinary actions of the participants more clearly.

We need not stop at the educational system, but could reduce the universe we are analysing still further and consider the school or the classroom group as social systems. This will be done briefly in a later chapter.

Structure and function

Structural and functional analysis of society is probably the most common approach taken by sociologists. It is, of course, an important approach, but not the only one. However, Davis has gone as far as to suggest that it is the only theoretical method which sociologists have developed in that ' . . . structural–functional analysis is sociological analysis' (123). Parsons' development of the social system outlined above is a structural–functional approach to the study of society. It follows in the line of a long tradition of sociological writers. In fact, in his book, *The Structure of Social Action*, Parsons tries to show that his work is the logical development of such writers as Durkheim, Pareto and Weber.

Mitchell (74) illustrates the functional orientation by reference to a statement by Voltaire, to the effect that if there were no God, man would have to invent one. This means that he regarded the belief in God as being functionally necessary to man. Using functional analysis, a number of writers, including people like Herbert Spencer, Radcliffe Brown and Malinowski, developed functional theories about society. As we have already mentioned in the discussion of the social system, all functional theories, including those of the writers mentioned above, suffered from an inability to explain change and conflict in the system. They were committed to a view of society which saw it as a stable system, in a state of equilibrium in which the most important functions were integration and the maintenance of consensus.

Merton tried to solve these problems by postulating some interesting concepts. 'Function', he defines as action which results in the adaptation or adjustment of the system to its environment, and goes on to refine this concept by suggesting that there are two main types. The first is MANIFEST FUNCTIONS. These are functions 'which are intended and recognised by the participants in the system' (71). The important point is that the participants are aware and intend consciously to achieve certain ends which are regarded as functional for the system, which may be a group, organisation or a society. This differs from what Merton calls LATENT FUNCTIONS 'which are neither intended nor recognised' by the participants. In other words, these are functions in the system which the members are simply unaware of as such.

He goes on to develop probably the most interesting concept of the three and that is the idea of DYSFUNCTIONS. These are actions which decrease or lessen the adaptation or adjustment of the social system. That is, behaviour which is non-adaptive for the system, such as most deviant behaviour. Like functions, dysfunctions can be either latent or manifest. From the point of view of the maintenance and integration of the university system as it exists at the moment, the activities of the radical student movement can be seen as dysfunctional, particularly their rejection of the existing authority structure and goals of the system. These immediately raise many issues, one of which is the relativity of what is functional and dysfunctional. Obviously, the radical students must view their activities as legitimate attempts to alter the *status quo*. In terms of their goals and values their actions are functional and those of the university authorities dysfunctional. The same relativity may be seen in industry where the activities of management might be regarded as dysfunctional in terms of the workers' definition of the system, and *vice versa* by the management. It is obvious that universities, schools and factories form groups of interacting people which do not share common standards and values yet we continue to regard them as systems.

It would seem, in fact, that the only values they do share is an equal acknowledgement of the influence of power and a preparedness to enter into actions which can be regarded as being either co-operatively oriented or oriented towards conflict. This suggests that a system comes into being when actors are prepared to inter-act with other actors over a period, within certain conditions, which can be questioned. This interaction can be either integrative or disintegrative as far as the system is concerned. In this view both consensus and conflict are admitted as fundamental processes in a social system.

SUMMARY

We have outlined certain basic concepts in sociology – interaction, roles, position, status, norms and values – and attempted to link them in a system. We have suggested that interaction is the basic unit of analysis for understanding behaviour, that actors occupy a position in a social structure, and that they play roles and acquire status. Furthermore, that during this process norms and values emerge which act as standards of behaviour for the actors, in that they have expectations about each other. These, in turn, influence their interaction.

We could present it in this way:

(INTERACTION) → (POSITION, ROLES, STATUS)
→ (NORMS, VALUES) → (INTERACTION)

This forms the basic elements of our system which, when analysed in terms of its structure and functions, reveal four functional subsystems. This is the functional – structural approach which has weakness in its inability to explain change and conflict. We suggest, however, that change and conflict form an integral part of the system.

NOTES

1. See Gould and Kolb (35), Mitchell (74) and Sills (90).
2. Mills (73), page 219.
3. Weber (100), page 112.
4. Weber (100), pages 115–18.
5. Johnson (50), page 4.
6. Broom and Selznick (10), page 68.
7. See Blake, J. and Davis, K. 'Norms, Values and Sanctions' in Faris (30), page 458.
8. Fallding (125), page 334.
9. Gross, Mason and McEarchen (37). See Part I in particular.
10. Merton (71), page 369.
11. Merton (71), page 370.
12. Johnson (50), page 2.
13. Johnson (50), page 4.
14. See Cooley, C. H. 'Primary Groups' in Hare, Borgatta and Bales (43).
15. Davis (19), chapter 12.
16. See Sherif, Muzafer 'Group Influences upon the Formation of Norms and Attitudes' in Maccoby, Newcomb and Hortley (63).
17. See Asch, S. E. 'Effects of Group Pressure upon the Modification and Distortion of Judgements' in Cartwright and Zander (13).
18. Merton (71), page 234.
19. Merton (71), page 229.
20. Adapted from Parsons, T. 'General Theory in Sociology' in Merton (72).

FURTHER READING

A well-established text book is Davis (19) which contains discussion of some of the basic concepts.

Johnson (50) is well set out with a particularly lucid discussion of functional aspects of the social system. Careful attention should be paid to the first three chapters.

Broom and Selznick (10) provides an excellent introduction to sociology containing adapted readings from many of the most important works in the field. The student should find this useful, the main drawback being that much of the material is American.

A recent text, containing useful information about contemporary British society, is Cotgrove (17).

Although a difficult book, Merton (71) is clearly written and contains essential reading in the first two parts for anyone wanting a deeper understanding of sociology.

3 The Family and Socialisation

We are not born social. The child is born knowing nothing of the ways of his society but having the potential to learn them. This process 'by which someone learns the ways of a given society or social group so that he can function within it' is termed SOCIALISATION.[1]

Elkin (25) and others have suggested three main prerequisites for socialisation. Firstly, there must be an ongoing society into which to be socialised. Secondly, the child must have the necessary biological potential. If, for instance, the child suffers from serious mental handicap then socialisation is difficult. Thirdly, the child requires the ability to establish emotional relationships or to engage in AFFECTIVE behaviour, as it is largely through such relationships that the process of social learning continues.

From the point of view of society, socialisation is necessary in order that it is able to 'perpetuate itself beyond a single generation' (25). From the point of view of the individual, socialisation is a process of learning and adjustment whereby he acquires the values, beliefs and behaviours which are both customary and acceptable to his fellows.

Socialisation is the process by which the child as a biological organism is given a sense of identity with the capacity to regulate his behaviour in relation to the surrounding situation. This *development of self-identity* is sometimes referred to as the *development of personality* or, as Everett K. Wilson describes it, 'answering the question for the newcomer; who am I?'.[2] The answer to the question involves the capacity for self-recognition or seeing himself as others see him which Cooley (14) describes as the 'looking-glass self'. It also involves the ability to take account of the expectations of other people regarding this behaviour or to the 'take the role of the other' (66). The child can only learn social behaviour of this kind by being in interaction with other people, and sociologists have always emphasised the importance of group experience of all kinds in facilitating this process. It is probably this aspect which most differentiates the sociological view of socialisation from that of *learning theory* and *psychoanalysis*. Learning theory tends to focus on the process by which learning, as such, takes place, independent of a particular environment. Psychoanalysis concentrates upon individual personality development through the study of significant emotional attachments. In stressing the importance of interaction within a patterned system, the sociological view should be particularly helpful in analysing all educational processes. Cooley (14) says, 'In these (primary groups) everywhere human nature comes into existence. Man does not have it at birth; he cannot acquire it except through fellowship, and it decays in isolation'. The primary group with its intimate face to face interaction has been described as 'the unit of all the social structure. It is the group which, in the form of the family, initiates us into the secrets of the society' (59). The human infant's long period of physical dependence upon others necessitates considerable time and attention being devoted to its care and upbringing. It is largely in the family that this takes place.

Most of us have had experience as a member of a family and, therefore, there is a tendency for us to believe, mistakenly, that we are an authority on family behaviour. This overlooks the fact that the family, though a unit to be observed universally, is a highly differentiated unit which varies significantly according to community, social class, economic development and other factors. Therefore, our experience within the family is only a particular view of a complex phenomenon.

What is more, because we have ourselves learned our social roles and attitudes within this particular unit, we have particular expectations of the variety of social positions and social situations which confront us. These particular expectations will not necessarily be in accord with the expectations of those with whom we have to interact. Students of education will be concerned with the socialisation of children who may come from varied social situations, different from their own. It is, therefore, vital to understand more of the variety of family patterns which exist and their effect upon the child. By describing the effect of different family forms in other societies, anthropologists can highlight the importance of variations within our own society (to which we must restrict our attention for reasons of space).[3]

THE FAMILY SYSTEM IN RELATION TO THE SOCIAL SYSTEM

Sociologically the family is a social system located in the larger, more comprehensive, and more complex social system which we call society. We have already emphasised the importance of the inter-relationships between parts of a system and between one system and another. Bell and Vogel (6) suggest that the relationship between the family and society could therefore be described in terms of a number of functional interchanges, 'In these interchanges, the external systems regard the NUCLEAR FAMILY as a corporate, separate unit'. The family can be seen as having interchanges with the four sub-systems of society:

1. *The family and the economic system*
Here the modern family usually exchanges its work or skill for monetary remuneration in the form of wages or salary. Until recently this was largely through the head of the household but is now increasingly through the contribution of others, e.g. the wife. This exchange is usually regulated through 'conditions of employment' which may increasingly be institutionalised by statute or contract. Special organisations, like trade unions, have emerged to co-ordinate and integrate the needs of the worker and his family in relation to the power of the industrial corporation. The family has to subordinate itself to the demands which the worker must meet in participating in the interchange, e.g. in his place of work, hours of work, and his holidays. In consumption, the family interchanges its assets, usually money earned in production, for consumer goods. The availability of such goods is usually determined for the individual family by the economy. The requirements of families in the mass do, however, affect the

economy but through the techniques of advertising and mass persuasion these requirements can be manipulated.

The fact that the family within a modern industrial society is completely dependent upon interchange through the economic system for the satisfaction of most of its wants, and for the means of satisfying those wants, results in an accentuation of the importance of the economic and the material in the external relationships of the family in modern society.

2. *The family and the political system*

The family in our system is involved in the political process through the entitlement of the adult members to vote. The government provides a stable system within which the family can function. The family supports the régime through compliance with the policies. In modern society the government and the family are closely linked, e.g. through the protection of property, the marriage contract, the supervision of children's welfare and the maintenance of social security.

3. *The family and the integrative system*

Families need in some way to be integrated within the society. The sub-system concerned with this need is any system of affective relationships which surround and involve the family. These may be close, as in a stable well-integrated community, or diffuse and nebulous, as in many modern urban situations. They will involve functional interchanges, varying from the closely structured mutual obligations of the 'neighbourly' community, to the casual and fragmented assistance at times of crisis which may be typical of suburban life. It is through these interchanges that the family establishes its identity and provides for its stability. It is this system of affective relationships surrounding the family which, by acting as a reference group, largely determines its adherence to group norms and largely decides the norms to which it will adhere.

When any group develops and there is interaction taking place within it, then different social positions emerge and these social positions are evaluated by the members. We find the same process within a society. The evaluated rankings of a society and the formalising of such rankings into a stable structure is referred to as SOCIAL STRATIFICATION. In certain traditional societies the evaluation is based upon age, in others upon power and the access to power, for instance, through the ownership of land or wealth. In such a society birth largely determines a man's social position in a self-perpetuating stable social structure. In a differentiated specialised modern society the evaluation is mainly based upon the contribution which is made to the ongoing functions of the society. It is, therefore, largely based upon occupations and these are ranked hierarchically in the society. The ranking is determined by the importance of the function to the society, the length of training and skill required to undertake it and the particular responsibilities attached to it.

There is evidence to show that people mainly classify themselves into one of two broad groups, namely, working class or middle class. This differentiation is a subjective evaluation based upon occupation, prestige, income and style of life. This rather imprecise differentiation of social groups is not sufficient in sociology and various measuring devices are used to render it more precise. In Britain the Registrar General's is the most frequently used classification. In this, the working population is arranged into the following small number of broad categories called social classes:

    I. Professional, etc. occupations
   II. Intermediate occupations
  III. Skilled occupations
  IV. Partly skilled occupations
   V. Unskilled occupations
  VI. Unclassified

In this book we are only concerned with social stratification in its relationship to those aspects of education which we choose as examples. In this respect the effects of social stratification are largely mediated through the family in its interchange with the economy. The occupation of the father determines the ascribed social class of the child and this, together with the style of life of the family, determines access and response to education. Educational performance largely determines occupation and the achieved social class of the new adult.

4. The family and the cultural system

It is in relation to the values of society and to its cultural heritage that we return to the specific process of socialisation. The family is the smallest social unit responsible for preserving and passing on the values of the society. The wider society stipulates standards and, in the interchange, the family accepts them and arranges their continuance through socialisation. Similarly, the family conforms to the social values in interchange for social approval. These values are mediated by the local reference group as indicated in the previous section and therefore the importance of understanding the affective relationships surrounding the family is emphasised.

THE FAMILY—CHANGES IN STRUCTURE AND FUNCTIONS

The family is often said to be breaking down. People who make such statements usually have an idealised picture, based on the past, against which the modern family is judged. Viewed sociologically, the family can be seen as changing in its structure and functions because of the general process of DIFFERENTIATION and specialisation which is taking place within advanced industrial societies, and which affects the family through the interchanges described in the last section.

Changes in structure

The nuclear family of parents and their children is a universal social phenomenon, but in many societies it is subordinated to, or incorporated within, a large familial structure. Murdock (77) analysed 192 societies and found that 47 normally had only nuclear families, while 53 had POLYGAMOUS structures and 92 had some form of EXTENDED FAMILY. Advanced industrial society with its demands upon all sectors of society to move further and more frequently in search of education, training, jobs and housing is disrupting the elaborate close network of kinship relationships upon which the composite family structures depend. Therefore, although research studies show that after physical separation from the family of origin there is usually an attempt to maintain some measure of affective linkage, nevertheless the degree of control and immediate support exercised by the larger family group has usually diminished.[4]

The trend, therefore, is for the nuclear family to emerge as the most characteristic form of family structure. This trend has been accompanied by a general pattern of fewer children per married couple. Thus, during the last hundred years the mean family size has declined from just over six children to just over two. There have been fluctuations in this general trend as, for example, the 'bulge' of 1946 and 1947 and the period from 1956 to 1964 when there was a noticeable increase of births each year. Since 1964 there has been a decrease in the number of births each year but it is too early to decide whether this, as Kelsall puts it, 'marks the beginning of a new phase, or is merely a temporary halt in a secular upward trend'.[5] He describes how the climate of opinion favourable to smaller families originated in the upper and middle classes and spread because of the desire to maintain higher standards of living, and to improve the education and the social and economic position of the children. This is a good example of the results of the interchanges affecting the internal organisation of the family, as described in the last section. Kelsall also says:

And many other influences were at work, including the decline in religious belief, the spread of scientific attitudes of mind, the weakening of the family as an economic unit, the growth of urban living and the emancipation of women.[6]

Another important structural change is in the stability or permanence of the family measured through the incidence of divorce. This has increased thirty-fold since the beginning of the century but, taking account of legal separations with maintenance orders and an increase in the number of married people, the true ratio should show a three-fold increase (17). However this is not necessarily indicative of a decline in the importance of marriage and the family as an institution but rather a consequence of those structural changes which put more strain upon the marital relationship. This is described by Bottomore:

In these (i.e. non-industrial) societies, marriage is entered into as an economic arrangement and in order to have children (for economic and religious reasons) and not simply for the satisfaction of sexual needs; moreover it has the support of a wider kinship group, and the personal satisfactions of the two individuals who marry are not unduly emphasised. In some Western societies, and especially the USA, a combination of monogamous marriage, a rigid Puritan ethic which strongly condemns pre-marital and extra-marital sexual relations, and an ideal of romantic love, has established a mode of the marital relationship which is impossible, perhaps to realise.

After mentioning the limitation of family size, he continues:

Thus the marriage bond is reduced to a simple relation of mutual attraction, and this is less strong than the network of economic ritual kinship interests which unite the family in other societies.[7]

Changes in function

The last quotation refers to changes in the function of the family. Ogburn has suggested that five of the six family functions were being transferred to other agencies, namely, the economic (except as a unit of consumption), the protective, the recreational, educational and religious. The sixth, the affectional, he suggested was still centred on the family and the future stability of the family would depend on its strength.[8] Burgess and Locke (11) described the change of functions as 'from institution to companionship'.

Whereas the loss of many of the traditional functions of the family might suggest a decline in the need for it as an institution, the evidence of the higher proportion of the population who are married and the high level of the birth rate indicates a continuing desire for marriage and for children. There would seem to be strong forces maintaining the family as an important primary unit. Veness (98) showed that for the majority of British school-leavers marriage is an important objective and, particularly for the girls, not necessarily a long-term one. Parsons and Bales (85) emphasise that the modern family is a very specialised agency in modern society having two main functions:

1. The socialisation of children.
2. The stabilisation of adult personalities.

and to these Bell has added

3. The satisfaction of ego-needs (i.e. the needs for the individual to obtain emotional satisfaction from the giving and receiving of meaning and importance in interaction with another person).[9]

This specialised agency in modern society is based on what Winch (107) has called the 'core-relationship of father–mother–child'. He says, 'this trio of relationships constitutes the nuclear family. Then we may view the extended family as an elaboration of the nuclear family'. Zimmerman (113), in differentiating three forms of family based on the amount of power vested in the family, suggested that the change has been from the *'trustee'* family in which all the social life of the members is vested and which is ruled by the extended family, through the *domestic* family which is transitional and ruled by the church, to the *atomistic* in which the individual is all-important and responsible to himself rather than to the family group. For the atomistic family the ruling body is the state. The interest in Zimmerman's analysis here is in the suggestion that the modern family requires a great deal of support from the wider social organisation.

Elizabeth Bott (8), in her researches into the British family, suggests that the organisation within the nuclear unit is largely determined by the presence or absence of the surrounding network of relationships.

It is with these suggestions in mind that we approach the analysis of the family in our contemporary society.

THE FAMILY IN CONTEMPORARY BRITISH SOCIETY

In the last section we emphasised that the family as a social system in interrelationship with a wider social system which is rapidly changing is itself undergoing change. Families respond to change differently. They differ in their external relationships with the wider social system and, therefore, also in their internal organisation. Different families provide different socialisation experiences. It is essential for the student of education, who is also concerned with the socialisation experience, to understand these differences. Increasingly, education is given the responsibility of preparing young people for their future role as parents and citizens, and it is necessary for the student to recognise the variety of roles and functions which are involved. To simplify this process we shall suggest that the variety of family forms in our society can be seen as a continuum from a traditional family pattern of the extended family type to a modern family pattern of the nuclear type. In the following sections, 'profiles' of these two types are constructed, based on the work of a number of researchers.[10] The student should recognise that these are generalised abstractions or what Max Weber referred to as 'IDEAL TYPES'. The patterns may never exist in the pure and extreme form described here but should be seen as an aid in isolating the differences.

The traditional family

This family pattern is typical of stable traditional communities such as villages, small towns and settled working-class districts of large urban centres. These communities are not affected readily by social change because of the ongoing nature of their relationships which are not often disturbed. In these communities the nuclear unit is part of a wider familial structure comprising a close network of affective relationships with relatives and kinsfolk. The nuclear unit is usually established close to the family of origin of one or both spouses and it is the family of origin which is often the main focus of the network. In such a family pattern the nuclear unit is an 'open' system with many relationships across the boundary of the nuclear system. The members of the nuclear unit are often orientated outwards towards parts of the wider familial system for much of their social life.

1. *Leadership*: We are dealing with the leadership or goal-orientated sub-system first, because this is the sub-system concerned with decision taking and there must be a decision prior to the establishment of a family unit. We have already raised the question as to why marriage is important today. In this pattern it would seem that marriage and the home are synonymous. To the woman, marriage represents security, escape from work, and escape from the supervision of parents. The man hopes for comfort, independence and has a desire for a home of his own. Love is rarely mentioned as a reason for marriage and the desire for sexual relationships is not regarded as a good or sufficient reason for marriage. The need for companionship and the desire to have children are given high importance in the decision to marry. Often young people are inspired to consider marriage because of the

D

social pressures and loneliness arising when friends in the peer group begin to pair off.

The choice of mate is probably limited. Most people seem to marry someone socially like themselves. Rodman (88) suggests that those who are most like each other socially are the members of the same family but that the incest taboo almost universally precludes sexual relations or marriage between mother and son, father and daughter, or brother and sister. This incest taboo would seem to perform an important sociological function by eliminating sexual jealousy and rivalry within the nuclear family. By forcing the members of the nuclear unit to direct their sentiments outward to other units, Rodman suggests that it helps to maintain social solidarity and the exchange and development of social ideas and techniques. We therefore find that EXOGAMY is almost universally practised with regard to a person's nuclear family. At the same time, ENDOGAMY is usually practised with regard to one's larger social group. This means that a person usually marries someone from the same social group. When one selects a mate who is like oneself in a number of characteristics thought to be important, then this is HOMOGAMY.

In the pattern of the traditional family mobility is usually limited or non-existent and thus the choice of mate is limited. This mate is usually met in a public place – street, dance hall, cinema, public house or café. The first meeting is often insignificant or chance and develops into a regular association for reasons which subsequently are hardly remembered.

During courtship, men assume a more positive role and are more likely to be influenced by physical attractiveness than women. In a considerable number of cases, initially the women will dislike the partner they eventually marry. The courtship proceeds with no strong feelings and lasts approximately two years. Marriage is entered into often as a means of attaining status. Many of the women have repressed infantile ideas of marriage which supported by the stories in romantic women's magazines, lead to exaggerated expectations of the married state, thereby increasing the need for subsequent adjustment.

Choosing where to live depends largely upon economic factors and the policy of local housing authorities. The desire of the woman will be to settle down as near as possible to her mother and her female relatives, in a house as like as possible to the one in which she grew up. A house of familiar design in which the purpose of the rooms are suited to the family way of life is thought most desirable. In this aspect of the decision-making the wife often assumes leadership.

There will be considerable variation in sexual relationships within the marriage, but the man expects to decide when intercourse shall take place and to determine when children shall be born. The man tends to be dominant and possessive, expecting intercourse as part of the marriage contract. On the whole, women are less interested in sexual intercourse and a large number are dissatisfied with the sexual side of marriage. Much marital unhappiness arises from the different expectations of the men and women with regard to sexual intercourse.

Children tend to arrive early in the family pattern, not so much because of ignorance of family planning, as because of reluctance of the man, who in this sphere is the decision-maker, to use contraceptive methods. It may well be that the contraceptive pill, which puts a planning method firmly under the control of the woman and which has no physical limitation upon the sexual act, may have a fundamental influence upon family planning.

2. *Task allocation*: The man is not expected to help in the house. He is a shadowy figure with an important and established status within the house based upon his responsibilities outside it in work. The wife is expected to maintain the house, look after the children and do the shopping. The woman sees housework as her field of work and uses it as a therapeutic activity. Myrdal and Klein (81) suggested that in future women may see their home-centred role as only a limited phase during child-bearing and child-rearing, before returning to a role outside the home in work or voluntary effort. As in the future our economy will rely heavily for an increase in productivity upon an increased contribution of married women to the labour force, there may have to be significant readjustment to the role-expectations of women. In Gorer's study (34) men ranked good housekeeping first in importance of qualities in a wife, personal qualities second and understanding third. Five of the ten qualities ranked first referred

to the wife as housekeeper. This would seem to be the major part of the role of the wife in the eyes of the husband. Women in the same study placed understanding first, thoughtfulness second and a sense of humour third in the qualities they expected of a husband. The husband as a provider and father was only ranked tenth in the list. There is significant evidence here of a change in expectations after marriage on the part of both the husband and the wife. The husband tends to emphasise INSTRUMENTAL qualities in the wife after marriage, whereas he emphasised EXPRESSIVE qualities before marriage. These instrumental qualities are directed towards the goals of the family as an efficient housekeeping system. The wife, on the other hand, while before marriage interested in those qualities in her future husband instrumentally directed towards the goals of the family as an efficient economic or status-earning unit, changes after marriage to emphasise expressive qualities concerned with the internal integration of the family as a system.

The reliance on the instrumental leadership of the wife in matters concerning the family as a housekeeping unit is reflected in the husband's attitude to domestic financial arrangements. He gives a consistent proportion of his weekly wage to his wife and sees no requirement to divulge the total amount to her. He keeps the remainder for his personal expenditure and for occasional family treats and holidays. This financial independence has been shown by Townsend (97) to be considerably reduced in old age with consequent drastic effects upon the status of the man in retirement. Meanwhile, however, the man does not expect to know how the housekeeping allowance is spent by the wife and he does not expect to be involved in decisions of this kind.

There are important aspects of this allocation of tasks which relate to the administration of social security and welfare. Many families are judged upon the success of the man in his instrumental role in relation to the economic system whereas, for the family as a system, this may be of less significance than his expressive qualities with relation to other members of the family. Similarly, failure to manage domestic finance may be due to the tremendous responsibility which in this family pattern is carried by the wife who may be least suited to assume such responsibility. This family pattern, however, does not provide protection for her until mismanagement actually occurs and by then it may be too late for the husband to help. The man will take over the wife's duties in a dire emergency but otherwise his participation in the domestic activity of either housekeeping or child care will be minimal.

3. *Integration*: Usually the members of a group are integrated within it by the pursuit of common activities together. In this way the group builds up a sense of 'belonging'. The group develops a culture or 'style of life' which differentiates it from other groups so that the members feel part of an 'in-group', as distinct from the 'out-group'.

Families build up this 'we-feeling' by ritual activities at times of festivity or at times of crisis, e.g. weddings, funerals, birthdays. In the traditional family pattern it is in this sphere that there is the most noticeable influence by the surrounding network, because social inter-relationships of members of the nuclear unit frequently cross the boundary of the nuclear unit into the network system. In effect, it is the network which becomes the 'in-group' rather than the nuclear unit itself. The wife in the nuclear unit, because she has set up home near her family of origin, will continue to find most of her social relationships with the female members of her own network. Often this social life will be focused upon her mother who she will see regularly and frequently. Much of the family ritual will be network ritual and will be based upon the family of origin. The man of the nuclear unit will find his social life outside the family in the immediate community, usually in public sporting places or public houses with male friends, often those who he knew before marriage and those with whom he works. The social life of both man and wife tends to continue the pattern it followed before courtship intervened and each tends to pursue a largely separate social life.

This is yet another aspect of what Bott has described as the SEGREGATED CONJUGAL ROLE of these families in which husband and wife have clearly defined areas of responsibility in which the other has little or no involvement. Segregated activities tend to limit the need and opportunity for discussion about the quality of the activity. Therefore, language in such a family is often limited to a comment upon physical activity. This limitation upon oral communication, a normal integrating process, makes the communication of problems more difficult when crises do occur. Many problems within families of this pattern are not verbalised and, therefore, are not capable of the same kind of solution which would recommend themselves to more articulate groups. Decision-making is difficult and arbitrary because of this lack of communication. This relates closely to the work of Bernstein who describes such patterns of communication as depending upon a 'restricted code' of language in which the qualitative aspects are very limited.[11]

The favourable aspects of marriage are seen by both men and women to centre around the children but, because both man and woman are orientated outwards from the nuclear unit towards the wider network of social life, then the social life of the nuclear unit itself is limited. Co-operation between the couple and 'give and take' are emphasised and considered much more important than the sharing of interests. The involvement of the adult members of the nuclear unit with the children of the nuclear unit is also limited and this has an effect upon the socialisation pattern.

4. *Socialisation*: Until the child can walk, its training will be completely in the hands of the mother. She will tend to be heavily influenced by folkways and traditional attitudes because of her close involvement with her mother and kinfolk. The support of the network will provide an 'in-group' which will be resistant to new methods of child care. Discipline will often be arbitrary and, as Kohn (130) has suggested, based upon the 'consequences' of actions rather than upon the 'intent' of these actions. Children will, therefore, tend to operate within the limits of arbitrarily applied sanctions without necessarily fully understanding the reasons for such sanctions.

Because of the close surrounding network and the familiarity of the environment, together with the involvement of the mother with her own social relationships within the adult network, there will be a tendency for the children to be encouraged, as soon as possible, to find their social relationships with their own age-group, either inside or outside the family. Play will be largely peer-group orientated and the child will spend a great deal of time outside the family in local situations with other children.

Involvement with adults will tend to be during visits or family gatherings which will be adult-focused, when the children will be expected to conform to adult requirements. Discipline, when applied, will often be severe and based upon corporal punishment. The father will often be regarded as the disciplinarian of the last resort and the one who administers the severest punishment. Studies show that children from these families, when questioned during adulthood, remember the father as an authoritarian figure, and as more domineering and agressive than the mother.

As this family pattern is usually rooted in an area in which there is extemely limited mobility, then there may be little evidence of parental ambition for their children. Aspirations tend to be confined to those which are realistic within the immediate social environment. Horizons will usually be restricted to the local situation and satisfactory adjustment to that situation is seen as the goal of socialisation (12, 65).

The modern 'nuclear' family

This pattern is typical of those social groups which have a tradition of mobility in search of training or career, such as the professions and the higher echelons of industry and commerce. In such families the establishment of the nuclear unit is almost inevitably at a distance from the family of origin of one, if not both, of the spouses. Due to the 'homogamous' tendency within social groups, it is likely that the spouses will have followed similar patterns of education, training and career and quite often, therefore, each spouse has already broken away from the familial network prior to marriage. It is also quite likely that they themselves have grown up in a similar nuclear unit which had broken away, at least to some extent, from the familial network. Even if this was not the case, then the nature of continued education and professional training is to some extent disruptive of the network in itself. Interests and attitudes are likely to develop which are different from the familial network and, therefore, the 'in-group' is likely to be one of professional acquaintances rather than kin-folk. So the spouses are likely to have a socialisation experience which has prepared them to establish a separate unit independent of the network. This unit tends to develop as a 'closed system' focused upon its internal relationships, rather than the 'open system' just described.

1. *Leadership:* While the occupation of the man is of obvious importance in providing for economic stability and for the conferring of status within the wider social system and determining the 'style of life' of the family, it does not earn for him superior status within the family system itself. Neither is there, necessarily, an assumption that the decisions which are orientated towards the external system, for example, where to live or whether to move in search of promotion, are exclusively his province. Decisions tend to be joint and based upon mutual discussion, during which as much information is provided as possible by both parties. All aspects of the family system are seen as entering into all decisions. While leadership may be assumed by one partner or another in a particular sphere of activity, it will be leadership based upon a commonly agreed policy. This is a particular example of what Bott has described as JOINT CONJUGAL ROLE in which most activities are shared equally and which is typical of the organisation of this nuclear family pattern.

2. *Task allocation:* Major responsibilities within the family organisation may be assumed by either partner. The man's professional competence will be supported by his wife's interest in, and understanding of, his functions. She may share directly in these functions as a kind of secretary, or indirectly as a hostess and confidante. The woman may develop a professional career in her own right and will receive similar support and advice from her husband.

Domestic management is largely an area for the woman but there is joint discussion and, in many of the activities, she expects participation by the husband. He may assume the initiative in certain areas of domestic responsibility. Similarly, the care and disciplining of the children will be seen as a joint responsibility and the man shares in the physical care of the child even during the early years, although it may be the main concern of the woman. In all areas of task allocation within the family, the tendency will be to see either partner as interchangeable with the other partner in as many functions as possible.

3. *Integration:* The essence of this family is that it is a 'closed'

system which conducts the majority of its activities together, as a unit, thus building up a strong 'in-group' feeling. This is partly due to necessity, in that being separated from its network it is thrown upon its own resources. Therefore, it builds up strong inter-relationships within the system in the absence of close affective relationships with the outside world. It is also, however, a matter of choice, in that the husband and wife will really believe in the importance of the nuclear unit and will support those theories of child rearing which demand a great deal of parental involvement with the children. The social life of the nuclear family will tend to be conducted as a unit, with parents and children participating equally in the activity. For this reason, much of the social activity of the unit will seem to be child-orientated or child-focused. Social relationships with adults outside the family will usually be conducted on the basis of shared interests and similar needs, rather than pursued as a matter of tradition. Therefore, relationships will tend to be with other nuclear units of a similar kind and with similar priorities. These relationships will not, therefore, threaten the 'closed' system but will enable it to thrive through occasional interchange with other similar 'closed systems'. As all activity of the family is conducted upon the basis of discussion and joint decision, and as much of the social activity of the family is conducted as a unit in interchange with other units, the degree of inter-communication within the unit is high and has to embrace the whole range of human relationships. The language used, therefore, is extensive and includes the qualitative aspects. The language in this family is what Bernstein calls 'the elaborated code', providing the members with the opportunity to describe the whole range of their experience.

4. *Socialisation:* In the nuclear family, because the social life tends to be focused within the 'closed' system of the unit of parents and children, the interaction between the members of this group is high. This, in turn, builds up a strong 'in-group' feeling which results in a high degree of involvement of each member with the others. The adults, both husband and wife, see child rearing and socialisation as one of their most important activities. A great deal of the *raison d'être* of the family is vested in the children. The children will be involved, as soon as they are

able, in the decision-making and discussion within the family and a great deal of the family activity will be child-centred. Discipline will be undertaken by either parent under an agreed policy and will usually take the form of rewards or the withdrawal of rewards. The reasons for decisions will be carefully explained and control of actions will be based upon an analysis of motivation, or, as Kohn puts it, the 'intent' of the action. The child is, therefore, socialised to develop self-discipline based upon internalised standards. Because so much of the family activity is child-centred, and because of the absence of a close and familar network, there will be less spontaneous peer-group play and involvement, especially in the early years. Play will be more consciously guided and directed towards social and educational development. The different social inter-relationships of the two 'ideal types' can be illustrated diagrammatically, as in Figure 2 and Figure 3.

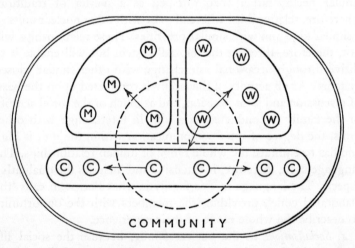

Figure 2 'Traditional' family – showing segregation within 'open' nuclear unit and involvement of individual members with different parts of community network.

We have already suggested that these two 'ideal types' are merely extreme generalisations of a variety of forms seen as a continuum. We should, therefore, look at one or two of the variations which can arise.

Firstly, writers have differentiated between the 'rough' and the 'respectable' in the 'traditional family' (54). In simple terms, this could be described as a differentiation between those families which are firmly vested in the mores of the 'traditional' pattern and are resistant to influences from outside the group patterns, and those families which are aspiring to the goals of groups outside and are adapting the 'traditional' pattern to accommodate those outside influences as, for example, in the adoption of standards of decoration, furnishing, entertaining and in educational aspirations for their children. The 'respectable' family could be said to have a 'reference group' of the 'nuclear family' pattern while still preserving the mores of its own culture. We are suggesting that these patterns of family organisation are a function of the closeness and stability of the surrounding network. Therefore, although we have described the traditional pattern as largely a working-class pattern, there will be many middle-class families which are organised on the traditional pattern because of the closeness of the surrounding network. In this case, the traditional pattern will be modified slightly by differences in the style of life of the middle-class family, for example, in education.

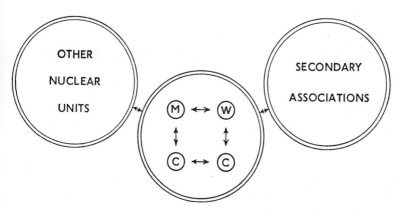

Figure 3 'Nuclear' Family – showing highly introverted interaction within closed system and relationship with other systems.

Similarly, there will be families within the working class which, because of the demands of modern society, are forced to leave the close network in search of job or housing and have to learn to develop the nuclear family pattern. This might be described as

The 'transitional' or 'emerging nuclear' family

Josephine Klein (53) has set out the changes in the style of life of such a family as follows:

1. from a close-knit family network to a more loose-knit one;
2. from a community-centred existence to greater individuation;
3. from a community-centred existence to a more home-centred one;
4. from a community-centred existence to greater participation in associational life;
5. from a segregated-role relationship to greater partnership in marriage;
6. from traditional occupational choice to social mobility;
7. from status assent to status dissent (That is, a change from a tacit acceptance of the traditional mores and an inward-looking lack of concern for 'out-group' issues to a concern to break the traditional pattern and to become interested in social change.);
8. from ascriptive values to achievement values;
9. from financial stringency to greater affluence;
10. from an emphasis on the bread winner to an emphasis upon the child.

Finally, it is necessary for us to recognise the existence of

The 'deprived' family

Klein (53) also clearly describes the existence of certain sub-cultural groups within our society whom she calls the 'deprived'. These sub-cultures have their own values and norms relating to family organisation and socialisation. These affect their patterns of courtship, sexual behaviour and marriage and result in a gap between their behaviour and the expectations of the wider society. This accentuates the insecurity which seems to be a dominant feature of their life and affects all their relationships with the wider social system.

The 'breakdown' family

Also, as we have suggested earlier, the removal of the nuclear unit from the close network surrounding it exposes the smaller unit to the stresses and strains of modern social life. Our modern welfare state is developing a variety of services designed to provide support for the nuclear unit. Often these services meet many of the needs provided for by the close network, for example, home help services and family welfare clinics (104). Nevertheless, the nuclear unit shows a greater tendency to break down under stress, and to develop stress symptoms which are not so readily concealed as they might be in the close network situation. This increases the need for planned social policy to take account of the effects of social change and for a study of the sociology of deviance (21). These are subjects with wide implications for education and will be investigated in the next chapter.

Before we do this, however, we shall provide a more detailed model of socialisation which the student can now accommodate to the different family patterns which have been described.

THE STAGES OF SOCIALISATION

Since one of the major objectives in the socialisation process is learning to participate in social roles and since, as already indicated, self-awareness depends upon an awareness of others, then it becomes apparent that an individual is required to internalise a *system* of roles which impinge upon his own role – as well as internalising his own role.

The model of the socialisation process presented here outlines four stages from infancy to adulthood. In all these stages, but particularly in the first three, the family is the main socialising group. At this point, it is therefore important to consider the roles of the dominant figures in the family unit, namely, the mother and father, and their role differentiation. The work of Zelditch on the nuclear family indicated that in most societies the father adopts the 'instrumental' leadership role in the family and the mother that of 'expressive' leadership.[12] This differentiation of role according to sex is very important in socialising boys and girls into the appropriate behaviour for them.

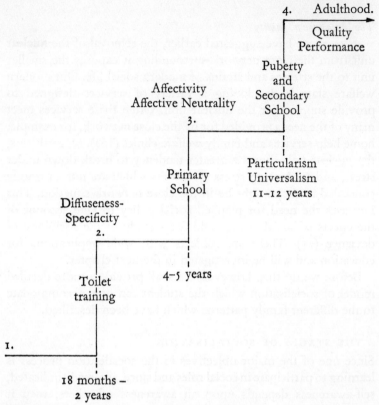

Figure 4   Stages of Socialisation

Our model (Figure 4) may be described as a series of plateaux with each new level being reached after the child has adjusted to the demands of the new situation. It is also a model which must not be seen as being of universal applicability but rather as one which approximates to the general process to be found in Western industrial societies.

Included in the model will be 'pattern variables' – possibilities of action which face anyone entering into a new situation.[13] The selection of one or other of the possible courses of action will, to a large extent, depend upon the previous pattern of socialisation which the child has undergone – past experience will largely determine one's perception of a new situation and also the action deemed to be suitable. These 'pattern variables' are arranged in pairs. The first pair is DIFFUSENESS – SPECIFICITY which pertains to the fact that an 'occupant of a role, in his interaction with another person, may have strictly limited and specific obligations toward that person or he may have an indefinitely large number of obligations . . .'.[14] The pattern variable AFFECTIVITY – AFFECTIVE NEUTRALITY deals with the permitting of certain kinds of expression ('affect') in certain situations as opposed to the controlling of this affectivity. What the child has to learn is that one must sometimes forego the expression of affectivity and the pleasure this may give in order to achieve certain ends. UNIVERSALISM – PARTICULARISM is the pattern variable which covers the situation in which the individual finds that there are certain rules and regulations which apply to all who participate in that situation (universalism) and that he, as a particular individual, cannot expect these rules to be bent simply on his account. The pattern variable QUALITY – PERFORMANCE refers to the emphasis which may be given to what an individual can do and how well he does it irrespective of his characteristics (qualities), such as age, sex, status or wealth.

The first stage of the process is one during which the infant is completely dependent upon the care and attention necessary for his survival. In most families it is the mother who attends to his needs and, yet, ' . . . if the father or anyone else shares with the mother the task of caring for the baby, no role differentiation is involved: that person will also be performing the role of "mother" '.[15] This lack of awareness of the role of differentiation by the infant means that no pattern variable is involved.

Stage two begins after what, to many children, is often a period of considerable disturbance. This is caused by the demands placed upon the child to exercise some control over itself, particularly in respect of toilet training. When some measure of control is achieved, the child is really into the second stage during which an important development occurs. This is the increasing awareness by the child of the mother as a separate being – the first 'significant other'. During the first stage, the child when aged about six months is able to recognise its mother (or whoever else may fulfil the mothering duties) as someone distinct from others. But this is different from what is happening in the second stage, for now the child is becoming aware of her as a person in her own right and not merely as an extension of itself. During this stage, the growth of the strong emotional and even physical ties between mother and child are prevented from going too far by the existence of an incest taboo – some form of which exists in every known human society. The relevant pattern variable is 'diffuseness–specificity'. The child is beginning to perceive the specific aspects of the mother's activities, such as the treatment of injuries and the provision of meals. In return the child extends a diffuse love.

The second stage in our model comes to an end at about four or five years of age with the entry into school. This entry into the wider world is accompanied by the introduction of the pattern variable 'affectivity–affective neutrality'. Prior to this time children are often encouraged to be outgoing and affectionate, but now, as a result of the diminished supervision by the family, there is often an exhortation to be rather less outgoing. This may be exemplified by the injunctions to the child not to accept sweets or rides from strangers. A further demand is placed upon the child at this time in that it must now accept that self-control is important – that very often it must forego an immediate pleasure in return for a deferred gratification.

This move out of the family into the school is the third stage in the socialisation process. Increasingly, the child is learning that other people also have to be considered and that he is no longer the rather special (particular) individual he is at home, and that other's wishes cannot be disregarded. The essence of this differentiation is expressed in the pattern variable of 'particularism–universalism'. One of the clearest ways in which this may be seen is by watching children at play. Piaget (87) says that children below the age of seven or eight cannot participate in 'true' games – that is, games which have universalistic rules. The essence of universalism is that the basic 'rules of the game' ensure that each player, whoever he may be, will have exactly the same rights and obligations as the other players. Mead (66) also considers this theme to be important and draws a distinction between a play stage and a game stage. He sees the socialisation process in three stages. The first stage lasts up to two or three years of age during which the child copies the activities of others without understanding their meaning. The second (play) stage is that in which the social character of the 'self' is revealed because the child's conception of self conforms to the way it is conceived by others, or, to put it another way, the child is now taking the 'role of the other' in relation to itself. But, as the child's social environment widens, so the number of 'roles of the other' it has to take increases. This can lead to the child developing a 'series of discrete selves, wavering and perhaps inconsistent'.

It is in the third or game stage that Mead sees a more or less consistent self-conception emerging. He uses the word 'game' to express the need of the child to reconcile diverse expectations and to meet common ones; instead of taking the role of *the* other, he must take the role of *all* others, the 'generalised other' as Mead calls it.

The onset of puberty and entry into the secondary school marks a period of great change, both physical and social. There is a further emerging from parental control and influence with the peer group becomes of immense significance in the life of the young person. Musgrove's (80) study of young people in Britain revealed that two-thirds of his sample of nine-year-old boys wished to have their parents with them on a day's outing, whereas at fifteen only one in forty expressed the same wish. Here the pattern variable is 'quality-performance'. During this stage, there is increasing pressure placed upon the young person to be independent and to make his own decisions. Increasingly, he is assessed by others on the basis of what he does, rather than what he is. This emphasis upon achievement rather than upon ascription is further reinforced by the gradual movement of British society from an ascription-orientated to an achievement-orientated society. But one of the dilemmas facing adolescents in Britain is that there is no clear definition by adults of their role. In many pre-industrial societies there are often clearly defined stages of preparation and initiation into adulthood, whereas for the adolescent in Britain there is a series of different ages for marrying, for driving a car, for voting – stages along the route to adulthood (98, 24, 26).

E

SUMMARY

The family is seen as undergoing change from a composite familial pattern to an independent 'closed' nuclear pattern. At the same time, it is shedding many of its traditional functions while still retaining its fundamentally important function of the socialisation of children. These two trends are making more necessary the network of services supporting the family. Education is an agent of continuing socialisation and is a system charged with responsibility to prepare young people for the responsibilities of socialisation. As such, educationalists must understand clearly the variety of patterns and their consequent effects. These are seen as ranged on a continuum between the two 'ideal types' of traditional family and nuclear family. The importance of the relations of the family with the surrounding system is seen as crucial.

NOTES

1. Davis (19), page 195.
2. Wilson (106), page 98.
3. For instance, see the work of Mead (67, 68, 69, 70).
4. Research studies conducted into the family and community relationships of modern British society, such as those of Young and Willmott (105, 111, 112), Mogey (75), Jennings (49), Townsend (97), Rosser and Harris (89) and the article by Litvak (134).
5. Kelsall (52), page 23.
6. Kelsall (52), pages 18–19.
7. Bottomore (9), pages 171–2.
8. Ogburn, W. F. 'The Changing Functions of the Family' in Winch (108).
9. Bell, Robert R. *Marriage and Family Interaction* (Dorsey Press 1963), page 8.
10. These include those mentioned in note 4 with the addition of Gorer (34), Slater and Woodside (91) and Klein (53).
11. Bernstein, B. 'Social Class and Linguistic Development' in Halsey (40). Also see references in chapter 5.
12. Zelditch, Jnr., M. 'Role Differentiation in the Nuclear Family' in Parsons (83).
13. Parsons (86), chapter 1.
14. Johnson (50), page 136.
15. Johnson (50), page 125.

FURTHER READING

A useful outline of the process of socialisation can be found in Elkin (25).

Klein (53) provides an excellent summary of research into the contemporary British family. The second volume, on child rearing practices, is of particular interest to students of education.

Downes (21) summarises most of the cultural theories of delinquency and gives a useful indication of research.

See Erikson (26) for some useful articles on the general question of the adolescent in modern society. This is an aspect of socialisation which particularly concerns the teacher.

Willmott (104) gives an outline of the major social services and could be used by the student of education as a guide to the supporting services to the family.

4 The Educational System

This chapter is concerned with the educational system and we shall select some aspects which illustrate the interest of the sociologist in education and not elaborate on aspects which are best dealt with by philosophers or educationalists. Sociology should be concerned with the relationship between education and society and, as an example of this interest, we examine briefly the relevant works of some sociologists. We have selected some of the earlier and more theoretically orientated writers because they have, to some extent, influenced the development of the sociology of education, and also because there is a marked contrast between their more speculative work and modern empirical research. Whereas the latter tends to be narrow and concerned with particular problems rather than with the total system, these classical writers were concerned with wider issues. In many respects concern with the relationship between the educational system and society is an aspect of the sociology of education which has failed to develop and one which should be given more consideration today. Their work is particularly appropriate as an introduction to an analysis of the educational system.

SOME SOCIOLOGICAL VIEWS OF EDUCATION

Herbert Spencer (1820–1903)

Biographical background: Spencer and Auguste Comte are usually regarded as the founders of sociology. Spencer was born into a middle-class family in Britain. He had a non-conformist upbringing and was educated at home by his father. Thus Spencer, like another great contemporary of his, J. S. Mill, was educated outside the conventional school system. This, in part at least, must account for the strong doctrine of individualism he was to put forward later. He wrote a phenomenal amount and in 1862 published the first volume of a series of books in which he set out to 'unify all the theoretical sciences of his day'.[1] This immense task covered areas such as biology, psychology, sociology and ethics, all of which were dealt with in nine volumes; besides these he wrote many other books and essays, among which are four review articles on education written early in his career.

Spencer's sociology: Spencer developed a universal theory of evolution, the essence of which was that there was always a movement from the simple to the more complex. He sees evolution as the integration of matter 'during which the matter passes from an indefinite, incoherent homogeneity to a definite, coherent heterogeneity . . .'.[2] In the development of all things, including societies, there is this movement from the uniform to the multiform, and increasing differentiation and specialisation. For Spencer, evolution was a slow but progessive force.

In addition to this doctrine of evolution, Spencer contributed to the idea that society was, in many respects, similar to an organism. Society, like an organism, grows, develops special structures and functions which are inter-related, forming a 'nation of units' of which the whole might be destroyed while the parts continue to live. There were some differences: in an organism the parts exist for the benefit of the whole, in a society the whole exists for the benefit of the individuals (the parts); in an organism consciousness is located in a specific area (the brain), whereas in a society consciousness is spread or diffused throughout the system.

Spencer's sociology of education: In his view the functions of the educational system must be minimal. This *laissez-faire* image of society leads to an educational process which stresses the role of the individual. In this sense he precedes John Dewey and much contemporary educational theory; education is seen as an individual learning and experiencing process. Spencer believed that one should not interfere with what he considered to be the natural processes of society. People had a natural propensity for freedom and society would progress without any interference. His educational theories rest on the same assumption of non-interference; he proposes that nature provides us with a sense of what is painful and pleasurable and, therefore, acts as a guide to how we should behave. A child will learn by suffering the consequences of his actions, and this is nature's way of 'teaching' the difference between right and wrong. This same principle is applied to parental behaviour, in that parents should teach the child by taking advantage of the natural likes and dislikes of children. For example, children dislike parental affection to be withheld, and he recommends this as an effective means of getting results.

Spencer sees the relationship between the educational system and the society as an organicist would – he says, 'There cannot fail to be a relationship between the successive systems of education, and the successive social states with which they have co-existed'.[3]

All the parts of society are inter-related and the educational system reflects the general pattern of society; all institutions in a society, he believes, have a 'family likeness'. He shows how an autocratic society is reflected in a corresponding type of educational system and how, with increasing liberalisation of the society, the educational system will develop similar liberal tendencies.

What is the relationship between society, the educational system and the individual in this theoretical system of Spencer's? In his essay on moral education he says, ' . . . educational systems, like political and other institutions, are generally as good as the state of human nature permits'.[4]

This fits with his overall view of man and society: the state of society and the educational system being determined in the last resort by the nature of man, which in turn is subject to change according to the laws of evolution.

Emile Durkheim (1858–1917)

Biographical background: This famous sociologist was born into a strongly rabbinical family in a small French town. He studied in France and Germany and was appointed to the chair of 'The Science of Education and Sociology' at the Sorbonne. His acknowledged master was another Frenchman, Auguste Comte, whose writings on the scientific study of society certainly influenced him. Comte was a positivist and, like Herbert Spencer, a believer in social evolution. It was Comte who first used the word 'sociology'. Initially, he had called the new science social physics, which more aptly reflected his positivistic approach. Durkheim reacted strongly against the individualism of Spencer and modified the positivism of Comte.

Durkheim's sociology: In *The Rules of Sociological Method* (23), published in 1895, he sets 'out to give a more precise statement of sociological facts and to establish the criterion of method'.[5] Durkheim believed that the phenomena sociologists should study were social facts and that these social facts were things. He defines a social fact as ' . . . every way of acting which is general throughout a given society, while at the same time existing in its own right independent of its individual manifestation'.[6]

By this, in marked contrast to Spencer, he is suggesting that a social fact, like a thing, has an existence external to the individual. For Durkheim, social facts are the means of explaining social behaviour and are not to be reduced to individual or psychological facts. This approach is sometimes referred to as *sociologistic*, and holds that society be regarded as something *sui generis*. This means that society is unique and has an independent existence, in this case independent of individuals. It would seem that society, in Durkheim's view, is the source of the individual and that the state of a society is reflected in the state of the individuals who are part of it. In *Suicide*, an excellent theoretical and statistical work, Durkheim shows how individual acts of suicide are related to the structure and state of society. He classifies three different types of suicide – egoistic, altruistic and anomique.

Durkheim's sociology of education: Although Raymond Aron refers to Durkheim as being 'condemned to teach a course in education',[7] it is obvious that Durkheim considered the study of educational institutions important.[8] Sherwood D. Fox in his introduction to *Education and Sociology* says, when discussing the value of this work, 'It is precisely the application of the sociological approach to education that makes these analyses useful to those interested in education from a practical point of view, as well as to sociologists.'[9]

This can, in fact, be seen as the fundamental function of the sociology of education and as Ottaway has correctly observed,

Durkheim can be considered 'the founder of educational sociology'.[10] Durkheim approaches education as part of his general sociology; it is a social fact and, as such, it is an 'essential element of his sociology'.

We have already noted that Durkheim felt that social facts were external to the individual; he also believed that social facts exercised constraint over the individual's behaviour. This element of constraint is of particular importance in education, as can be seen by his definition:

Education is the influence exercised by adult generations on those that are not yet ready for social life. Its object is to arouse and develop in the child a certain number of physical, intellectual and moral states which are demanded of him by both the political society as a whole and the special *milieu* for which he is specifically destined.[11]

Durkheim sees the role of education as fitting the individual into the social system, supplying the socially blank child with the appropriate norms, mores and customs to fit him into his social *milieu*. Education is a social thing both in its origin and in its function. He sees this social function in the following way: 'Society finds itself with each new generation, faced with a *tabula rasa*. . . To the egoistic and asocial being that has just been born it must . . . add another capable of leading a moral and social life.'[12]

Like Spencer, he saw the educational system and society as being bound up with one another and believed that society developed a system of education suitable to its own structure and epoch. He took this even further when he suggested that each social class, caste and locality, develops its own system of education, 'each occupation . . . constitutes a *milieu sui generis* . . . '.[13] This is something which most teachers would readily accept from their own experience and, in fact, recent educational reports are beginning to take these social differences into account.

The function of the educational system is to fit the individual into his social *milieu*, be it society or social class. If one is to educate so that individuals become suitable members of an existing society, can education bring about any changes in society? Durkheim saw 'educational change as dependent on more profound social change'.[14] It would seem that, in Durkheim's

view, the functions of the educational system do not inc
of changing society. It could be argued that the rela
between education and society is a two-way process but h
not suggest this in his writings. What Durkheim does sugg
that the education theorist should make it his task to bec...ne
aware of, and to advocate, social and educational change.

George Herbert Mead (1863–1931)

Biographical background: George Herbert Mead, was a philosopher and social psychologist of whom his close friend John
Dewey said '. . . the most original mind in philosophy in the
America of the last generation'. Mead was the son of a Yankee
parson, he studied in America and briefly in Germany, and later
lectured at the University of Chicago until his death. His only
major works are, in fact, posthumous publications of the notes
taken by his students during lectures. Fortunately, during his
life time, he published numerous articles among which are many
which reflect his deep interest in educational problems.[15]

Mead's sociology: Mead was a pragmatist and certainly influenced by the philosopher, Peirce, and the psychologist, James.
He developed a form of social behaviourism while trying to
show that the minds of individuals could be studied objectively.
C. W. Morris, in his introduction to *Mind, Self and Society*, sees
Mead attempting ' . . . to show that mind and the self are without
residue social emergents; and that language in the form of vocal
gestures, provides the mechanism for their emergence'.[16]

Mead set about achieving this by studying observable activities,
the on-going social processes, such as social acts, and showing
that mind and society arise out of this dynamic on-going process.
This concept of the self arising out of interaction with others is
one of the significant contributions which Mead made to social
psychology. Like Spencer and Durkheim, he had something to
say on the relationship between the individual and society. In
contrast to Spencer, he puts it this way ' . . . the whole (society)
is prior to the part (the individual), not the part to the whole; and
the part is explained in terms of the whole, not the whole in terms
of the part or parts'.[17]

What he is saying is that social psychology attempts to explain individual conduct in terms of the organised behaviour of the social group, and not to explain the behaviour or actions of the social group in terms of the individuals who are members of the group.

Mead sees the self developing in this social environment by internalising the roles of the other, initially through gesture, later through language. A person's image of himself develops out of what he imagines other people's attitudes towards him are. Eventually, the individual develops a more organised conception of the community's attitude towards him; Mead calls this the 'generalised other'. This internalisation of the attitudes of the 'generalised other' leads to the incorporation of the values and norms of the community into the developing personality.

Mead's sociology of education: The implications of Mead's theories regarding the development of the self are of the utmost importance for education. This is particularly so in the kindergarten, where the teacher can aid the child in his self-development through role-playing in game and play situations. This gives the child an opportunity to learn about rules, expand his awareness of others and his developing self. The relevance of play and game situations is recognised in modern education as it is something which 'lies entirely inside the child's own experience' and, therefore, can be easily utilised in the learning process.

Education for Mead is the attempt to get a 'social response into the individual'. He defines it as follows: 'Education is definitely the process of taking over a certain organised set of responses to ones own stimulation; and until one can respond to himself as the community responds to him, he does not genuinely belong to the community'.[18]

This definition firmly relates the educational process to the social *milieu* in which it is embedded, and is in many ways similar to what Durkheim was saying. A young gang member who rejects the educational situation in favour of his gang's norms, is responding to a limited 'generalised other' which is certainly not that of the whole community. On a wider level, politicians who respond purely in nationalistic terms, without seeing the role of the country in the international community, also have a limited 'generalised other'.

Education, as an institution, is seen by Mead as people responding in similar ways to particular situations. When a person enters an institution, like a school, he will be capable of adequately taking the role of others in the situation. This means he can respond to them and they to him as the situation requires. If we look at the case of the gang member, he either fails to, or does not wish to, take the attitude of the teacher in any interaction with him. He therefore defines his own role and that of the teacher in a way which is different from that of the other participants in the institution. This is a system of continual change; it is dynamic because it is based on the on-going process of social acts. Therefore, the society and the selves in it are continually undergoing change. This dynamic approach to behaviour can be of great value to teachers as they are dealing with a developmental process. Mead provides the teacher with a framework for the analysis of his own actions and that of the pupils in a reciprocal way, in the learning situation.

Max Weber (1864–1920)

Biographical background: Max Weber was born into a wealthy family of linen merchants and textile manufacturers in Western Germany. His father was a lawyer, who on moving to Berlin became a successful politician, and was for some time a member of the Reichstag. Weber senior was a national liberal whose house was frequented by many of the leading men in both political and academic circles of the time. With this background, it was not surprising that Weber was a precocious child and profoundly serious, never participating in sport or play and spending most of his time reading. He read widely, particularly history and, as a result, had a considerable knowledge of world history. He enrolled at Heidelberg University as a law student, studying economics, philosophy and history as well as the usual courses. In 1889 he obtained his doctoral degree, and a few years later accepted a chair at the University. A short while after taking the post he suffered a breakdown, and was unable to do any work at all for four years. Mills and Gerth note that during the rest of his life he suffered intermittently from severe depression, 'punctuated by manic spurts of extraordinarily intense intellectual work and travel'. It was on his return from a visit to America that he finished one of his most famous works, *The Protestant Ethic*. Weber was always deeply concerned about politics and came near to standing for the national assembly. This involvement in German politics is reflected in much of his writings, which were attempts to understand some of the problems confronting Germany at the time.

Weber's sociology: Weber's contribution to sociology is important and we can get some idea of how important when we note than an eminent contemporary sociologist, Raymond Aron, has said, 'To me, Max Weber is the greatest of sociologists; I say that he is *the* sociologist' (2).

All we can hope to do in this passage is to give the student an outline of some of the more important contributions made by Weber. Methodologically, Weber faced some of the same problems that Durkheim, Spencer and Mead had tried to deal with. One was to decide whether the social sciences could adopt the same techniques as the physical sciences. Weber saw the role of the scientist as that of arriving at *laws of causal explanation.* He believed that the social sciences and the natural sciences were different, but not all that different. He admitted that the subject-matter of social science, seen as the meanings and values which people held, was different from the subject-matter of physical sciences. Nevertheless, the sociologist could study these by developing a value-free perspective. Weber's sociology is an interpretative one. He concerns himself with understanding human action. This attempt at understanding human action is the main difference between the social sciences and the physical sciences. The physicist is not concerned with understanding the atom, or with what it feels like to be an atom, nor with the motives or meanings of events, but with the postulation of causal explanations and laws. The sociologist is concerned with understanding human action as it was purposely intended. It is this element of *verstehen* (understanding or comprehending) that is unique to the social sciences and can be regarded as an advantage over the natural sciences. This is a very different approach from that of Durkheim, in which there was no place for the subjective process.

Weber also developed the concept of ideal types which Timashaff (96) describes as being a mental construct, formed by exaggerating or accentuating one or more traits of observable reality. The ideal type which we construct can be called ideal because it exists as an idea. It is important to remember that ideal types are not real nor are they hypotheses; they are useful analytical tools which the researcher invents for analysing concrete historical situations or problems, such as, seventeenth-century Calvinism, twentieth-century capitalism, bureaucracy and rationality. In an earlier chapter we examined his concept of social action in which he distinguished four ideal types of social action. This use is repeated in his other works. We find, for example, in his political sociology a discussion of three types of authority. Firstly, there is the *rational legal* domination which is based on impersonal rules or norms and corresponds to zweckrational action. Secondly, there is domination which is based on *tradition*, having a sacred element in it and being similar to traditional social action. The third form of domination he calls CHARISMATIC, which is based on the devotion to the special inner qualities an individual leader might possess. It corresponds to the affectual form of social action.

In his writings on the sociology of religion, Weber tries to show that a special relationship exists between early capitalism and certain forms of Protestantism. He tries to show, by detailed analysis of a number of religions and their societies, that certain religious preconditions existed only in the west, which facilitated the development of capitalism.

Weber's sociology of education: Weber never wrote on the sociology of education as such, but a number of his works have an indirect bearing on education, particularly his writings on politics and science as vocations and some of his historical writings. We may examine educational systems using relevant concepts from his work. In the introduction to the translations of some of his work, the authors, Mills and Gerth, remark that, in contrast to the liberalism of some German and American writers on education, Weber's view is a pessimistic one. Weber saw education and the 'social production of personalities' as being dependent on politics and economics. They conclude that 'His pessimism about political and economic freedom is thus supplemented by his pessimism about the realms of art, cultivation, and the personality types possible for contemporary man.'[19]

A theme which runs through much of Weber's comment upon education is the differing demands that a changing social structure, particularly in the economic and political field, makes on the educational system. For example, as a society becomes increasingly bureaucratised, there is a shift from the educational ideal of the cultivated gentleman to the specialist and expert. This is expressed in his discussion of the 'rationalisation' of education and training. For example, he suggests that beneath all the discussions of the foundations of the educational system is the struggle of the 'specialist' type of man' against the older type of 'cultivated man'. This struggle is being determined by the 'irresistibly expanding bureaucratisation of all public and private relations of authority and by the ever increasing importance of expert and specialised knowledge'.[20] One of the consequences of this process is the decline of property as a basis for social differentiation and the rise of education to perform this function. In his discussion of China, Weber, in dealing with the educational system of the Chinese literati, develops the basis for a typology of education. He sees two polar opposites in the area of educational ends. These correspond, on the one hand, to charismatic structures of domination and, on the other, to the modern rational structure of domination, the bureaucratic. The difference is that in the charismatic form, the approach is to *awaken* something which already exists in a person. In the rational form, an attempt is made to *train* the pupil for a practical role, involving specialised and expert knowledge. Chinese education was neither of these two types, but tested, by a rational examination system, whether or not candidates were familiar with a body of classical literature.

In many respects these distinctions between two types of education and two ideals of the educated man are as relevant today as they were then. The recent report of the Fulton Commission (1968) on the Civil Service would seem to be concerned with these issues. Although in modern society it would seem that the issues have been decided in favour of the rational type expert, it is possible that some of the student unrest, and the move from the sciences to the humanities, suggests the search for another solution.

CHANGES IN THE STRUCTURE AND FUNCTION OF
EDUCATION

The situation external to the educational system may be seen as
being composed of two elements – the historical (past) and the
contemporary (present). An obvious but important difference is
that while both exert influences upon the contemporary educational system, it is only in respect of the latter that there can be
some measure of reciprocal influence.

An important function of the educational system is to contribute to the process of socialisation by transmitting much of the
culture of a society to each new generation. Important as this
function is, care must be taken to avoid seeing the purpose of the
educational system as only that of maintaining social cohesion
and continuity. While this may be largely true of the pre-industrial type of society, another function becomes increasingly
important in an industrial society – namely, to be an agent of
social change.

The characteristics of the educational system in pre-industrial
society are clearly set out in the 1953 *World Yearbook of Education.*

Under primitive conditions a tribe must hand on from generation to
generation its language and its ways of life as well as the skills which
provide for the daily needs of the community. Three levels of instruction are necessary. The young children must learn the tribal language
and the elementary rules of behaviour. The boy and girl must be
trained in the arts and crafts which are the basis of subsistence. Adolescents have to be initiated into tribal mysteries and taboos before they
are accepted as full members of the tribe. There are, of course, no
special institutions and no professional teachers to perform these
tasks. The mothers teach young children to speak and walk, to eat
and dress; they were kindergarten mistresses long before Froebel
invented the term. The fathers and male relatives teach the boys how
to fish, to hunt, to fight and to care for domesticated animals; they are
master craftsmen, the direct ancestors of our vocational teachers. And
the priests or medicine-men initiate the young men into the tribal lore
and culture; they are the precursors of our academic teachers in
universities and secondary schools.[21]

This passage contains a number of points which may be used
to illustrate some of the major differences between pre-industrial

and industrial educational systems. First, the amount of formal education given to children has increased. The above description indicates that most of the knowledge was transmitted in an informal situation and was largely utilitarian in nature. The formal element was largely reserved for the initiation by priests or medicine-men into adulthood. Most of the knowledge was remembered and passed on by word of mouth. The invention of writing allowed cultural preservation and transmission on a much larger scale. Associated with this was the emergence, even more clearly demarcated, of learned men, either sacred or secular, who were the preservers and transmitters of knowledge. Bryan Wilson (145) makes the point that they were 'not so much teachers as guardians of knowledge, and knowledge is esoteric, sacred, aristocratic'. The same writer goes on to say that in such societies knowledge was to be preserved but not expanded, and that its transmission was carefully limited to a select few who had been initiated into the ranks of the literati. In this, the educational process was indeed largely concerned with ensuring continuity and cohesion.

But signs of structural differentiation and functional specialisation can be seen in this. The existence of the literati indicates the existence of some specialisation of function – while the fact that the rites of initiation (and the necessary instruction) into either adulthood or the ranks of the literati often occurred in a place apart from the everyday life of the society, marks a degree of structual differentiation.

As a society becomes increasingly industrialised and complex and there is an increase in the division of labour and in social differentiation, the variety of roles into which the people must be socialised also increases. There is also a qualitative difference in that

... relationships are much less comprehensive and personal obligations are felt not towards a compact body of persons but towards people in their individual roles as close relatives and friends. In Western economic and political institutions, in particular, the whole organisation of activities tends to be based on loyalties of a largely impersonal and abstract kind.[22]

This means that the same formal education is not appropriate for all people in the society.

Differentiation and specialisation in British education

Bottomore (9) argues that before 1944

. . . the educational system can be broadly characterised as having provided elementary education for working-class children, secondary (grammar school) education for middle-class children, and public (fee-paying) education for children of the upper and upper-middle classes.

Such an arrangement reflected the tri-partite social structure of British society.

The public schools sought to inculcate in their pupils the qualities deemed to be desirable for those who were taking their place as leaders both at home and in the vast territories of the British Empire. 'Their emphasis was less with learning and more with leadership.'[23] The children from middle-class homes attended the grammar schools where the curriculum was aimed at turning out industrious, thrifty and loyal citizens who could take their place in the world of commerce and industry. But as the middle class became increasingly wealthy and ambitious, so their desire grew for their children to have the social advantages of a public school education. To meet this growing demand it was necessary to establish new schools, and almost a half of our present-day independent public boarding schools were founded during this time.

Along with these developments, efforts were made to extend secondary education to a wider section of the population. One result of this was a renewed interest in the grammar schools on the part of the 'lower' middle class – the traders and shopkeepers. Whether a grammar school was a new or a revived establishment, there was a general acceptance that many of the characteristics of the public school were very desirable and, therefore, should be incorporated into the grammar school. 'Thus it was that the shibboleths of education for gentlemen were transferred to the sons of traders, shopkeepers and artisans . . . '.[23]

But it is in the attempts to establish a national and compulsory system of education for all children that the importance of factors external to the educational system can perhaps best be seen. The government first entered into the field of education in 1833 by making grants to two charity school societies. Before

F

that, such schools as had existed for the children of the working classes, had been sponsored by the voluntary system which was essentially religious in its orientation. Two of the most famous societies concerned in this work were the National Society for Promoting the Education of the Poor (a Church of England society), and the British and Foreign Schools Society (a non-conformist society). The voluntary system arose as a response to the urbanisation which accompanied the industrialisation then proceeding apace in Britain. It sought to combat the 'breakdown' in the established religious, moral and social order.

Government intervention, however, had occurred earlier, but in a more indirect manner, in the Health and Morals of Apprentices Act of 1802 which stipulated some instruction for apprentices in the Three Rs. The Factory Acts of the nineteenth century also concerned themselves, to a limited extent, with the education of children. The 1833 Act, for example, stipulated that those children between nine and thirteen years of age should receive two hours schooling daily. This activity on the part of the Government resulted in the establishment in 1839 of a Select Committee of the Privy Council to deal with educational matters.

Attempts to establish a national system of elementary education with governmental support had been made prior to 1833 when bills, such as those of Whitbread, Brougham and Roebuck, had been introduced into Parliament. The influence and power of religious bodies at this time is indicated by the fact that these bills were defeated largely through their opposition. Their opposition to the growth of a non-sectarian system of education is further exemplified by their reaction to the suggestion, made in 1839, that the provision for the training of teachers be extended by establishing normal (i.e. non-religious) training colleges. In this case, their opposition did have some beneficial effect in that they increased their own training facilities by opening new colleges.

In 1862, there came into operation the Revised Code – so called because it radically revised the system established in 1846. Thut and Adams (95) write that this made very apparent the 'political control exercised by the upper classes over the Education Department' and that it 'perpetuated the stigma of charity which had always been attached to public funds for education'. Under the new code there came into being the famous 'payment by results' scheme, whereby the government grant to a school depended upon the pupils' attendance and their success in passing a standardised examination administered by the inspectorate. Furthermore, the grant was to be given to the managers of the school rather than directly to the school itself. Many other measures were introduced, aimed largely at cutting down the expenditure on education. So successful were these measures that the amount was reduced by some 30 per cent within a few years of their introduction.

With the introduction of Forster's Act in 1870, there came into being the dual system of British education. Under the terms of this Act, the Government instructed the Education Department to establish elementary schools in those areas not adequately served by voluntary schools. Although the implementation of this recommendation was left largely to local initiative (and consequently considerable regional disparities emerged), it resulted in a substantial increase in the provision of elementary education. 'The transition from a voluntary to a national system of education was led, step by step, by the extension of the franchise to the working people'. Only three years before had come the Reform Act which led to the working-class voters being of considerable influence in the balance of power between the Liberals and the Conservatives. Speaking in Parliament, Forster argued that 'now we have given them political power, we must not wait any longer to give them education', and that 'we must make up for the smallness of our numbers by increasing the intellectual force of the individual'. A hundred years later, we still hear this latter point being continually repeated.

The need for education to 'gentle the masses' was felt very strongly in nineteenth-century Britain, particularly when violent upheavals in other European countries, as in 1848, were seen to serve as a dreadful warning. In addition, Britain's lead in industrial development was being whittled away. The impressive efficiency of Germany's army and industry was looked at in the light of its educational system. There, a system of elementary education had been in operation since 1794 and, by 1871, less than 5 per cent of children were not attending school. This was compared with the situation in Britain where, for example, in 1870 the percentage of men and women signing the marriage registers with a mark and not a signature were 20 per cent and 27 per cent, respectively.

Following the increase in the provision of educational facilities came the move towards compulsory education. In 1880 attendance was compulsory until the age of ten; in 1899 until eleven, and then, in 1918, attendance became compulsory until the age of fourteen.

The Act of 1902 laid responsibility upon the local authorities to provide education for children between five and fourteen years of age. This was elementary education and was to be free and compulsory up to twelve years of age. At discretion of the authority it could extend up to fourteen years of age, but as mentioned, this did not become a national stipulation until 1918. Under this Act, the Government would also assist the local authorities in providing secondary or other higher education. This form of secondary education was not free. This, together with the fact that a selection examination was involved, meant that only a small proportion of working-class children gained entry into this level of education. It was not until 1944 that secondary education for all was provided and then the school-leaving age was raised to fifteen.

The persistence of a tri-partite system of education is worthy of comment. This idea was first propounded formally in 1868 by the Schools Inquiry Commission, which recommended the establishment of three types of secondary school in which the differences were to be based on the social gradings of the pupils. This is understandable when one thinks of the clearly tri-partite social class structure of Britain. The idea of education being used as a means of 'gentling the masses' and preparing children from different backgrounds to fit into their ordained positions in society was used to justify such an arrangement. This idea continued and the suggestion that there should be secondary schools of three types (grammar, technical and modern) was included in the Hadow Report of 1926, the Spens Report of 1938 and the Norwood Report of 1943 (148).

Durkheim's (22) definition of education as preparation to take one's place in 'society as a whole' and in the '*milieu* for which (one) is specially destined' seems to rest to a large extent upon this assumption. In this, education is seen as being of vital importance in maintaining the cohesion and continuity in society. The 1944 Act was of great significance in its attempt to propagate the idea of equality of opportunity and to substitute an education based on the Three As (age, aptitude and ability of the pupil) for an education based on the Three Rs (reading, writing and reckoning). But the persistence of the idea of a tri-partite system is indicated by the fact that, although the Act did not mention such an arrangement, in most cases its implementation resulted in the establishment of grammar, technical and modern secondary schools.

This brief account of the development of the British educational system allows one to agree with the following statement in the 1967 *World Yearbook of Education.*

In some circumstances education can be a strongly conservative influence, particularly in a highly class-structured society where it is mainly available to the social elite. But when education comes to be regarded as a human right, as it is now, when its gates are opened to a far larger proportion of the population, when the curriculum undergoes modernisation, and when the teaching profession becomes an upward mobility route for able people from lower echelons of society: then education turns from a conservative institution into a powerful agent for social change.[24]

As a result of the process of industrialisation, it can be seen that schools have changed both in structure and function – that is, there has been an increase in structural differentiation and functional specialisation. It has been indicated that in the pre-industrial type of society, education is largely concerned with transmitting a way of life which is relatively unchanging. In this, the educational system is itself relatively unchanging and passive and less concerned with bringing about change in the situation external to it. But in the more complex and differentiated situation existing in an industrial society, the 'model which seems most useful for describing the relations between education and society is of two systems each of which is functionally related to the other by feed-back mechanisms' (17).

One of the ways in which this feed-back can be seen is in the changes in the amount and nature of knowledge. In an industrial society the increase in division of labour involves an increase in formal education which is largely devoted to the transmission of empirical knowledge. This knowledge is not so much 'esoteric, sacred and aristocratic' as 'a circulating specie, the influence of which grows as it is circulated'.[25] With it comes an increased awareness of human ignorance as well as of human knowledge. Behind it are attitudes of doubt, criticism and inquiry – 'doubt replaces faith as the test of knowledge'. This spirit of inquiry is institutionalised within the educational system. At the level of college and university, the importance of research is given as a major reason for their existence – and universities cling tenaciously to the autonomy which is left to them. From the research carried out in these and other establishments, comes an increase in knowledge which can often be used for utilitarian ends. But also this new knowledge feeds upon itself and extends the frontiers of knowledge in a way which is not always predictable. At the level of the school, there is an increasing emphasis laid upon the pupils 'discovering for themselves' – an emphasis which to a large extent rests upon the asking of questions and the expression of rational criticism by the children. All this involves the educational system in preparing individuals for a changing, rather than a static, world.

THE EDUCATIONAL SYSTEM IN RELATION TO THE SOCIAL SYSTEM

We have already seen that it is important to understand the inter-relationships between a system and the wider social system, and this section is concerned with the interchanges between the educational system and the four sub-systems of society.

The educational system and the political system

Forster's plea in 1870 for development of the educational system in order to maintain national supremacy is reiterated in a number of sources today. Thus Blaug and Lauwerys say ' . . . educational planning must now, of necessity, be at least national in scope'[26] and Drucker also says ' . . . the supply of highly educated people (is) a decisive factor in the competition between powers – for leadership and perhaps even for survival. ... Educational development becomes a priority of national policy'.[27]

The story of the growth of a national system of education during the nineteenth century indicates the increasing intervention and control exercised by the state. This was achieved despite considerable opposition from the religious bodies and from the numerous adherents to the prevailing *laissez-faire* ideology. Each of the Education Acts is an example of state intervention, albeit tempered with the permitting of a considerable degree of autonomy to the local authorities. Even the Act of 1944, in requiring the provision of secondary education for all, did not specify the exact form such education was to take. The result was that considerable differences arose in the way the Act was implemented. This acceptance of some measure of local autonomy persisted in the Government's method of introducing the comprehensive principle into secondary education. Each local authority was required to submit its plans to the Department of Education and Science, and these were allowed to take account of local characteristics or difficulties. The integration of the public schools into the state system has long been a wish of many members of the Labour Government. To this end, the Public Schools Commission was set up to investigate the possible ways in which, if not integration, at least some coming together of the private and public elements in our educational system might be achieved. The overall pattern is one of increasing government control of education. In this respect, the significant thing about the postponement of the raising of the school-leaving age is that no element of discretion was left to the local authorities. This was a truly national decision. And in the final analysis, every decision concerning the British educational system is 'inexorably a political one'.

Having said that, however, we still have to ascertain the goals of that educational system. With this in mind, we quote from the report of the Robbins Committee (148) who were faced with a similar problem.

The fundamental question we have to answer is whether a system of higher education in the sense in which we have used the word 'system' is desirable. As we have said it is misleading to speak as if there were already a system in this sense. Higher Education has not been planned as a whole or developed within a framework consciously devised to promote harmonious evolution. What system there is has come about as the result of a series of particular initiatives concerned with particular needs and particular situations. There is no way of dealing conveniently with all the problems common to higher education as a whole.

Probably a similar comment could be made regarding the whole educational system of this country. The Robbins Report goes on to point out, however, that the large proportion of public finance which is provided in order to facilitate the development of education makes it necessary to have a plan for so important a system. If there were a written system, well co-ordinated and well planned, then it would be possible for us to ascertain easily the objectives of the system because these would be clearly stated. This is not possible, however, in our system at the moment because, as we have suggested, such a plan does not exist. Therefore, in attempting to find the objectives of a system, the sociologist would go to those aspects which are concerned with direction and with guidance and attempt to extract from official statements in reports, legislation and policy guidance those ends which seem to be most clearly emphasised within the system. We shall give a few examples of how this can be done.

Let us continue with the Robbins Report and see what indications this may give us of the aims of higher education, and then we might ask how far these also apply to the educational system as a whole. The Robbins Report lists four main objectives essential to a properly balanced system of higher education. It states that, first, instruction in skills suitable for playing a part in the general division of labour is important. The Committee suggest that this is sometimes undervalued or even ignored and they point out that in our times we depend to a greater extent than ever before on skills demanding special training. 'A good general education, valuable though it may be, is frequently less than we need to solve many of our most pressing problems.' Secondly, they state that the system should aim to produce 'not mere specialists but rather cultivated men and women'. They point out that if education is to be concerned with practical techniques, it should impart them on a plane of generality 'that makes possible their application to many problems'. Thirdly, they mention that 'we believe that it is the proper function of higher education, as of education in schools, to provide in partnership with the family that background of culture and social habit upon which a healthy society depends'. This fourth aim mentions explicitly the schools and wider educational system and it would seem that the other aims are equally widely applicable.

So in this very important report compiled seventeen years after the passing of the Education Act of 1944, there are stated certain of the aims of our educational system which would seem to emerge from an analysis of that system. Continuing this analysis of the other recent educational reports, the following aims emerge.

The comments included in the report of the Scottish Working Party on the linkage of secondary and further education (entitled *From School to Further Education* (148) and published in 1963) are worth quoting because they may be more true of the total educational system than they at first appear. The report states

. . . the traditional Scottish secondary-school course was one designed to provide a broad general education with a distinct academic bias and suitable, in the main, as a preparation for the professions; and this tradition was to a large extent continued in the expanded secondary education for the years after the War.

At another point they state that the Education Act

. . . by requiring that secondary education should be provided for all, created a new situation for the secondary schools. Hitherto they had catered for the abler minority; now they were required to receive all boys and girls over the age of twelve, at all levels of ability, and to provide for them a suitable secondary education. During the past fifteen years, many teachers have made real efforts to study the needs of their pupils and to send them out reasonably prepared for life.

These two quotations could, we feel, be taken as generally applicable to the educational system of this country. They refer to the conflict between the academic goals of the educational system up to the 1940s and the new goals imposed upon the

system by the post-war Education Acts. Continuing its analysis
of this same problem, the Report refers to an official memorandum
of the Scottish Education Department, published in 1955, which
stated the broad aims of secondary education as a means of helping teachers to tackle the problem of education in the secondary
school. The aims referred to in this memorandum were very
broad: first, the need to foster the all-round development of the
individual pupil, ensuring that education was concerned not only
with his intellectual attainment but with character building;
secondly, education should include a substantial element
of social and aesthetic training and should give due attention to
emotional and physical well-being; thirdly, there should be the
inclusion of a vocational element in the general course of study to
take account of the fact that the pupil is looking forward to his
future as a young worker; and, fourthly, education should be
prepared to enable the young worker to use his leisure hours
profitably. The 1963 Scottish Report, concerned as it was to
investigate transfer from school to further education, naturally
drew particular attention to the need to meet the vocational aim
of education but, nevertheless, also stressed the importance of
education for leisure and education for citizenship. The report
gives special attention in one section to the needs of the 'less able'.
It states '... broadly speaking the aims of the school in its work with
less intelligent pupils are no different from its aims with other
groups'. Later they go on to say 'Measured in these terms the
simple object of the school is to provide for the less able, as for
other pupils, what is vaguely known as "a good general
education" '.

In England at the same time, a committee under the chairman-
ship of Sir John Newsom was investigating this particular
problem of the 'education of pupils of "average" and "less than
average" ability'. The report of this committee (148), which was
published in 1963, has also given considerable attention to the
aims of education. This report suggests ' . . . the Schools will
need to present that education in terms more acceptable to the
pupils and to their parents, by relating school more directly to
adult life, and especially by taking a proper account of vocational
interests'. Here again the emphasis is on the vocational, but for

the first time, in our analysis, emerges a concern for relevance in the view of the parents and pupils, as well as in the view of the system. This is an interesting distinction to which the Newsom Report draws attention: namely, the distinction between the aims of the system and the aims of the pupils and the parents of the pupils. Just as the Robbins Report had done, this report also sees the need to investigate the economic argument for investment in our pupils. An important clue as to the ends of education in an advanced Western country is contained in the following statement from this report:

Besides, in the national economic interest we cannot afford to go on waiting. Others are already ahead of us. It is true that we start school a year earlier than most other countries, but there is no reason to assume that the majority of our children are ahead of other pupils at the age of fifteen when they leave school.

There is a suggestion here that it is more important to educate to compete with other countries than to educate for the needs of the individual.

It becomes interesting to ask what education is, for whom it is designed and who designs it? The Newsom Report, as we have already said, indicates the conflicts sometimes existing in the educational system between the needs of the pupils and parents and the needs of the system. What is it that results in a conflict of this kind? Who is it who decides that the educational system should be different in its aims from the wishes of parents and pupils? In a democratic society, the wishes of the members of the society should gain expression within the system but here is an obvious example where, at times, the formal system is out of step with the needs of at least some of the participants within the system. How far does a compulsory educational system make sense, when it is possible to describe parts of it in the way in which the Newsom Report does?

Too many at present seem to sit through lessons with information and exhortation washing over them and leaving very little deposit. Too many appear to be bored and apathetic in school.

One of the clues, of course, is provided in a further statement – 'Most of the distinctive courses which have proved so successful have, for understandable historical reasons, so far been designed for the abler pupils'. The statement goes on to emphasise that a rather different quality will be required in education in the future. 'These girls and boys must somehow be made much more active partners in their own education. Whatever their natural endowments they all need to attain self-respect and a reason for wanting to work well'. The Newsom Report emphasised that the aims of the educational system were changing from an assumption that the narrowly conceived academic goals of the system itself were the most important and that participating pupils had to be fitted to those goals, towards the realisation that the needs of the pupil seen in his social setting were of equal importance and that the goals of the system needed to be accommodated to him. The sympathetic understanding of these changes was expressed in the following paragraph from the report:

Most teachers and parents would agree with us about general objectives. Skills, qualities of character, knowledge, physical well-being, are all to be desired. Boys and girls need to be helped to develop certain skills of communication in speech and in writing, in reading with understanding, and in calculations involving numbers and measurements: these skills are basic, and they are tools to other learning and without some mastery of them the pupils will be cut off from the whole areas of human thought and experience. But they do not by themselves represent an adequate minimum education at which to aim. All boys and girls need to develop, as well as skills, capacities for thought, judgement, enjoyment, curiosity. They need to develop a sense of responsibility for their work and towards other people, and to begin to arrive at some code of moral and social behaviour which is self imposed. It is important that they should have some understanding of the physical world and of the human society in which they are growing up.

This need for 'realism' in education has been continued in the development of comprehensive education as a national policy. There is little doubt that, regardless of the educational merits or demerits of comprehensive education as a policy, underlying the decision of the Labour Government to introduce such a system, was the strong feeling that social conditions were at the root of many educational problems. The social differences which the Robbins Report mentions, and to which the Newsom Report refers were resulting in differences in educational opportunity in a way that was anathema to a Labour Government. Committed to the removal of social injustice and social inequality, it was obvious that they could not tolerate an educational system which was seen to be emphasising such injustices and such inequality. At the same time, they were interested in trying to promote social integration in the community at large and these two aims merged in the decision to promote comprehensive education. Therefore, we can now add to our list of the aims of education the important one of social integration which can be seen as one of the major objectives of the comprehensive system.

This principle to which we have been referring has been taken a stage further with the publication of the Plowden Report (148), concerned with the state of primary education. In this Report, attention was drawn to the particular difficulties encountered by pupils in the so-called 'priority areas'. These areas were seen as those suffering particularly from the inadequacies and inequalities already referred to in earlier reports. These were areas where facilities were lacking or where pupils suffered from the educational system. The report however, went further than to draw attention to the difference in the areas and in the provision. For the first time in this country, an educational report suggested discrimination in educational provision, not in terms of age or intellectual ability as in the past, but in terms of the social ability to benefit from education. What is more important, this report discriminated in favour of the less fortunate rather than in favour of the more able and more fortunate, as in the past.

Though we have not a national plan so far as education is concerned, it is possible by analysing carefully the statements contained within official reports and other official documents to perceive some objectives within the educational system.

Inevitably, these objectives are reciprocally inter-related with the political system. Education continues the process of socialisation begun within the family and is, therefore, irretrievably linked with the concept of the society which it is desired to produce. Education becomes an agent of social change, while at the same time responding to social change.

The educational system may, at times, be seriously out of step with needs of the participants because of organisational constraints which restrict flexible response to changing social needs. It may also be an example of the difficulty of providing for adequate two-way communication between policy makers and the recipients of the policy in a modern democratic system. If one of the aims of education is preparation for citizenship, then the educational system has a real responsibility for producing citizens who can participate effectively in a democratic process. The educational system is, therefore, an 'open' system with clear responsibilities and interests in all aspects of the wider social system. Students of education and teachers need to be widely concerned with 'diffuse' issues outside their own 'specific' system.

The educational system and the economic system

The close link between the economic and educational systems is well exemplified by the recent (1968) government cuts in public educational expenditure. One immediate consequence was the postponement for two years of the decision (made in 1964) to raise the school-leaving age in 1970. The belief in long-term educational planning received a severe jolt because short-term management of the economy was shown to be more important. Development plans for secondary education, for example, plans for school building and the supply of teachers, had been drawn up on the basis of the school-leaving age being sixteen. Whether the disturbance of these long-term plans is likely to be of final economic advantage has still to be seen.

Each of the major educational reports published during the last decade has been considered neither too revolutionary nor too impracticable. Yet only a few of the recommendations have been put into practice. In many cases a major reason has been lack of financial resources to meet the necessary expenditure. This emphasises both the reciprocity of the relationship between education and the economy and the fact that education must compete with other priorities of the social system for scarce economic resources. Etzioni (124), in providing a typology of societies, classified democracies as 'drifting societies'. He pointed out that one of their most important factors was a tendency to introduce structural changes only in a crisis and 'when broad consensus can be mobilised before action is taken'. Educational cuts can be understood in this context. Vaizey takes up this issue of consensus when comparing the educational programmes of Conservative and Labour Governments. After stating that both parties 'have created a remarkable atmosphere of consensus politics in education'[28], he argues that, for this to continue, long-term planning is essential and yet we have seen how this has to be related to economic considerations (127).

There is another more specific way in which the educational system is related to the economic system. We have already shown how a society evaluates different functions within the society and develops a system of social stratification. Our society is one in which achievement is replacing ascription as a means of placing people within the status hierarchy. The function of a person in the society, as measured by his occupation, is becoming much more important than his family in placing him in that hierarchy. This is connected with an increase in BUREAUCRATISATION which entails the necessity to conform to impersonal universalistic standards and these, in turn, generate a demand for efficiency or achievement. Therefore, as the amount of formal education has increased so has the importance of formal educational qualifications. This is associated with the increase in occupational specialisation in a highly-developed industrial society. Education is increasingly seen as the means by which achievement can be translated into social mobility. The teaching profession, for instance, has long been regarded as one of the clearest paths of upward social mobility for children from working-class homes. Modern society has seen a proliferation of other non-manual occupations and entry into many of these depends upon educational qualification (131, 133). In this process the structure and content of secondary education has been much influenced. The grammar or selective secondary school has been important in preparing children for upward social mobility (33).

As education as a grading agent for the system of social stratification has become increasingly important, so has grown the concern to discover the extent to which the education is socially biased.

Earlier research in the 1930s was directed towards disposing of the nature–nurture argument and then to trying to give the facts relating to access to secondary education. By 1945, it had been generally established that educational opportunity was much less for the children of the lower social group than for the children of the professional classes.[29] The impetus of educational reorganisation after 1945, however, did a great deal to eradicate this unequal access. Floud, Halsey and Martin (31) concluded in 1957 that the proportion of children of skilled workers achieving selective secondary education compared with those of the professional and managerial parents in schools in Hertfordshire and Middlesbrough were equitable, provided that measured intelligence could be assumed free from environmental influence.

This important proviso regarding the possibility of social bias in measured intelligence has emerged as one of the crucial problems of educational policy. There is increasing evidence that social environment has great influence upon educational attainment. There are also significant problems attached to the question of retaining within the educational system those whom wider access permits to proceed to continued education and of enabling them to achieve their full potential. We shall return to these questions in the next chapter (32, 128).

The educational system and the cultural system

At the same time as there is in society an increasing SECULARI-SATION and an increasing growth of knowledge and awareness of human power and limitations there is, almost paradoxically, a demand for the educational system (at least at the school level) to concern itself with the inculcation of certain standards and values. Our analysis of education in nineteenth-century Britain showed how the voluntary system arose to combat the breakdown in the established moral order. And, although at the present time the schools are less concerned with 'gentling the masses', the pressures from the external situation in this respect can be seen in the fact that religious education is the only mandatory subject in the curriculum.

This reflects the fact that formal education was originally conceived as having merely an ancillary role in the socialisation of the child. The 'moral welfare' of the child was earlier the only area of sufficient importance to justify the assumption of responsibility by the State. We referred in the previous chapter to the way in which functions of the family were increasingly being assumed by other services which develop to provide support for the more vulnerable nuclear family. The part played by the educational system in the whole socialisation process has become increasingly significant.

Under the influence of such writers as John Dewey progessive education has increasingly put emphasis upon the need to educate the 'whole child'. This includes the development of personality and of socially approved sentiments and attitudes, as well as the development of mental and motor skills. There is an assumption of the Rousseaunian promise of the 'goodness' of original nature in the child rather than the Puritan assumption of 'depravity'. Modern education therefore aims through a minimum of direction and restraint to encourage creativity and spontaneous expression (107).

Children are trained explicitly for adult roles, not only through vocational education but through courses in marriage, parenthood or family life. The variety of patterns and the likely need for adjustment of role expectations to which we drew attention in the last chapter, would seem to provide evidence to justify such courses. As one of the aims would seem to be to help to change attitudes, these courses would probably gain if they were based on group discussion in mixed groups of peers.

Schools are developing ancillary services such as medical counselling and guidance services. A recognition of the importance of environment and socialisation in the development of 'problem' behaviour is leading the educational system to an increasing interest in the therapeutic aspects of education, and social workers have been attached to a number of schools. The

G

school day lengthens with 'after-school' or 'extra-curricular' activities and schools provide facilities for homework and private study. The role of the family in socialisation is correspondingly reduced.

Yet, at the same time, we have already suggested that the development of the nuclear family with its child-centredness is resulting in an increasing interest in education and an increasing desire on the part of the family to be involved with the school.

These conflicting trends have to be reconciled. The educational system is beginning to be involved in the socialisation of parents through educational courses designed to introduce them to new educational methods, to help them with problems of child development and to prepare them for the family adjustment problems when the children reach adolescence. In this way, school and home begin to develop a partnership in socialisation and the inculcation of values. Whether the partnership is one in which parents can or should contribute ideas and information, participate in policy or influence change, is a particular aspect within the educational system of the general social question of alienation and participation.

The educational system and the community

Just as we suggested that the integrative function for the family system was fulfilled by its relationship with the surrounding community, so it is for the educational system. The educational system can be seen as concerned in an input–output or interchange process in which the educational units take in material from the community and, after a conversion process, pass out the material again into the community. The conversion process may, therefore, be either functional or dysfunctional to either the community or to the individual pupil, depending upon their particular requirements. Many educational issues can be clarified by applying this analysis to the relationships between the educational system and the community. To illustrate this we have constructed a model, as shown in Figure 5.

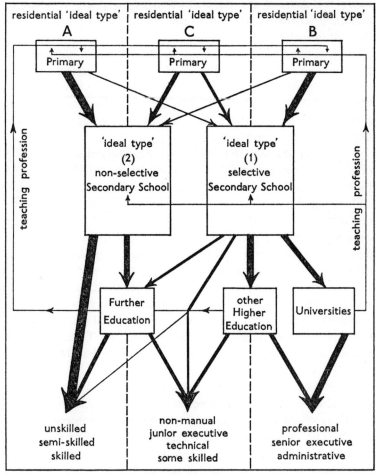

I N P U T

Figure 5   Flow Diagram of Educational System

The components of this model are as follows:[30]

1. *Primary schools*

It is a basic assumption of planning within modern communities that the primary school should be seen as the neighbourhood

school. It should be built within a catchment area which mini-
mises the distance and the traffic danger for young children in
attending school. At the same time, modern housing policy and
the attitudes of house-owners are resulting in the development of
residential areas which are homogeneous in types of house and in
the socio-economic background of residents (111, 112). Our
model suggests that the primary school reflects the homogeneous
socio-economic nature of its catchment area. The model contains
three 'ideal type' primary schools which correspond to the three
family areas described in the last chapter.

The traditional school: In this school the catchment will be largely
of children from the traditional family pattern. (Ideal type A.) As
the area is stable and unchanging, the building will often be old
and designed for a by-gone era. Because of priorities within the
rest of the system the ratio of pupils to staff will be higher than
elsewhere in the system. Teachers who are produced from another
part of the system will be disinclined to teach within this part of
the system, and there will be a more rapid turnover of staff than is
normal and a greater proportion of inexperienced teachers. There
will be a leavening of strongly motivated teachers who consider
education in this part of the system to be a social priority. These
teachers will often be frustrated due to the factors already
described and will, therefore, be less effective than they would
wish (Plowden 148).

The child will be socialised due to the traditional family pattern
and will expect to behave permissively within arbitrary external
sanctions which will be accepted as authoritative consequences of
action. The interests of such children will be spontaneous and
their goals will be short-term. They will be unlikely to show a full
understanding of the principle of DEFERRED GRATIFICATION.
They will have a restricted code of language and they will not
have much experience of close adult–child interaction. They will
be peer-group orientated and will have learned to see women as
'child care' or 'expressive' figures, and men as 'instrumental'
figures. Men will also be seen as authoritarian and disciplinarian.
This will have implications for the role of the teacher in the
traditional school.

There is some doubt as to whether the principles and policy of

the educational system are designed with this school in mi
Such a school could continue to apply an autocratic system of
arbitrary sanctions based on an authoritarian discipline and, therefore, continue the familar socialisation pattern for the child and so
meet his expectations. Or the school could choose to counter the
socialisation pattern within the family and prepare the child for
participation in an individuated nuclear society where sanctions
are largely a matter of internal choice.

If the school takes the first solution there is difficulty in
reconciling this with the progressive education and the demand
for spontaneous and free expression which are stated aims of the
system.

If the school takes the second solution it will need to be prepared
for the conflict which will arise during the stage when the expectations of the pupil are not being met by the system. This stage,
during which new socialisation patterns are learned within the
school, may be a lengthy one for the pupil. As the school is
continually receiving a new intake, it will be a continuing problem
and will impose considerable strains upon teachers and upon the
school.

The strain will be greater because there will be conflict between
the socialisation patterns and values of the school and those of
the home.

The school will have great difficulty in communicating its
policy to the parents. There will be little or no parental involvement in the education of the children. The attitudes of the parents
may vary between a tolerant but negative attitude based on lack
of understanding, and an apathetic withdrawal or suspicious
resentment (57).

In such a school, it may be that progressive education has in
any case to be interpreted differently. A peer-group orientated
child with 'restricted' language may gain less from being encouraged to participate in group activity with others of a similar
background, than in greater adult-child interaction which would
widen social experience and language.

This would require a higher staff-to-pupil ratio than is normal
in order to maximise adult-child interaction. 'Project work' and
'discovery' methods might have to be organised differently when

there is not a favourable home environment for self-directed work. The employment of specialised auxiliaries and the development of facilities for pupil research may be more necessary within this school than within other types of school in the system. The Plowden Report (148) has made suggestions of this kind for socially disadvantaged areas but it may be that the need is wider than that envisaged.

The progressive school: The catchment of this school will be largely from families of the stable nuclear pattern. (Ideal type B.) Being in a well-established residential area the building may be old, but the priorities of the system will have resulted in it being modernised and provided with additional facilities. The same priorities will result in a lower ratio of pupils to staff than in the previous type. Teachers will wish to teach in this school because of the acceptability of the raw material, the progressive methods and the 'results' which will increase professional status. Staff turnover will be small and the school will develop a consistent policy. The teachers will be in accord with the policy of the school and there will be little conflict or frustration. At the same time, this school has an in-built problem in that the stability and consistency and the higher proportion of older, experienced teachers may result in resistance to innovation and change. This will be overcome if the strong motivation of the staff can be utilised to encourage support for in-service training and refresher courses at which new methods can be introduced. It is an encouraging feature that the educational system is beginning to recognise the need to build in to the system a means of providing for on-going change.

The children within this school will be socialised to participate in decision-making and to control their behaviour by a concern for the motivation of their actions. They will have an elaborated code of language and their style of life will accentuate experiences which are supportive of the educational aims of the school. The home background will include access to books, museums and wide social experience (20). In many cases these children will already have begun the socialising–educational process within a nursery school or play-group. This is due to the fact that parents in these areas appreciating the need for, and benefit from, nursery education are often providing such experience by joint effort.

This is an indication of how the whole socialising experience of these children will prepare them for the progressive methods of education and it would seem that the principles and policy of the system have been largely developed with them in mind. Having had considerable interaction with adults, they are ready to assume responsibility for their own actions and will benefit greatly from being stimulated to peer-group activity.

The parents will largely be from the professional or executive groups and will usually have had continued secondary education and often higher education. They will value education for its own sake but also as a means of achieving social status. Though they will have no experience of modern educational methods, they will be aware of them through reading and will be concerned to acquaint themselves more fully. They will welcome involvement with the school and will support parent-teacher associations and educational classes designed to help them to understand the educational and developmental problems of their children.

The 'transitional' school: This will usually be found in a new housing development, such as, housing estate or a new town. (Ideal type C.) The building will be new and designed for the most progressive methods of education. In certain cases the design of the building may be ahead of educational practice and may provide adjustment problems for the staff. The staff and Headmaster may be largely new and consequently there may be difficulties in developing policy and goals within the school. In many cases the building will be inadequate in size for the population in the catchment area and classes may, therefore, be large and this may hinder educational practice. There will be a tendency for the staff to be young and enthusiastic but they may live mainly outside the area and for this, and other reasons, staff turnover may be quite high. Nevertheless, the school will usually be using progressive methods and have the best facilities and equipment.

The families from which the children come will largely be of the 'emerging' nuclear pattern of mobile working-class families who have been separated from their network. They will contain a large number of 'status-dissenters' who have a middle-class reference group and who have aspirations to higher status, if not for themselves, then for their children. They will see education as a means of upward social mobility for their children. At the same time, they will be adjusting their own roles and their family organisation. This may result in inconsistency and insecurity, and cause difficulties in the socialisation of the children and the relationships of the family as a system with other systems, such as the school.

There may also be a certain mixture of lower middle-class families in which the achievement of the father has not matched his potential or his aspirations and results in what Swift (141) has called 'mobility-pessimism' or dissatisfaction with his job and prospects. These families will have a high commitment to education through the transmission of the frustration from the father to the children.

This school will find parents who are very interested in, and very conscious about, the school performance of their children. They may be suspicious of the progressive methods which they see as 'play' and unlikely to gain for their child the educational success they see as important.

Whereas the traditional school has the greater challenge as an agent of social change, the transitional school has the greatest opportunity to assist in the socialising of parents. It is the school which requires to be most supportive of the vulnerable nuclear family and has the greatest need to understand the changes to which we drew attention in the last chapter. To do this in the midst of an area often manifesting insecurity, it needs stable organisation and to project a consistent policy. Sometimes this is difficult when a school is establishing itself and is somewhat insecure.

2. *Secondary schools*

This book is being written at a time when great changes are taking place: the elimination of selection methods at the end of primary schooling and the introduction of a comprehensive system of secondary education. Our model is designed to illustrate the problems which were components of the previous separatist system and which, it suggests, still underly the new system in this transitional stage.

Secondary schools were previously not sited with the same

area or neighbourhood considerations which have been the case with primary schools. Secondary schools have emerged in certain situations by historical and social accident and, in the previous separatist system, could be differentiated educationally rather than geographically.

The 'academic' or 'selective' school: This school had a specialised intake based upon a process of selection. This selection could be on the basis of fee-paying, social suitability or intellectual ability, or a combination of them. Obviously, the first two criteria are directly associated with socio-economic status but even though they have been removed from the state sector of the educational system, there is evidence to suggest that socio-economic background has had a significant effect upon selection for academic education (20). Though the educational system provided equal access to selective secondary education, the opportunity to take advantage of the access was still unequal, as we have shown in an earlier section in this chapter. Our model, therefore, suggests that the greatest opportunity was presented to the output from the progressive school where background, facilities, methods and attitude were all favourable, and the least opportunity to the output from the traditional school where these factors were largely unfavourable. In the transitional school, that portion of the output which was closest in background and attitude to that from the progressive school would be most likely to succeed in the selection process (60).

The school was designed to produce good academic material suitable for entry to higher education and to the professions. The emphasis in the school was, therefore, upon academic achievement and the use of techniques designed to act as incentives to achievement, such as examinations and syllabuses.

The staff of the school were people who themselves were trained in this process and had been successful within it. They were identified with the process and had vested interests in maintaining it. They succumbed readily to the pressures within the system to refine itself by extending the curriculum, increasing specialisation and improving the academic content of the subject-matter. The academic process and the academic goals were all-important, and the pupil was seen mainly as raw material for the process and as successful output of the process. The teacher is seen as a subject specialist and as an academic expert. Personal relationships within the system are seen only as necessary to facilitate the academic process. The need for the teacher to understand the pupil in his social content or to relate the external situation of the school is minimised.

This will present no difficulties in so far as the selection process has largely resulted in an input which will readily identify with the system, assimilate the goals of the school and understand the process. But the input is also likely to contain at least two other minority groups.

First, there will be the small group from traditional areas who have succeeded in overcoming the social obstacles to selection but whose reference group is not the same as that of the majority of the pupils. They will exhibit what Swift (141) has called the 'direct' level of culture clash, in that their values and goals will be in direct conflict with the school. These are the 'non-conforming' pupils, the 'early-leavers' or 'drop-outs' who are unsuited culturally to the process in this form.[31]

Secondly, there will be the small group, probably from transitional or traditional areas, who have succeeded in the selection process, but who have a social background and socialisation experience which does not give them sufficient support or understanding to realise their full potential, even though they seem to be conforming to the process. These are exhibiting culture class at the 'latent' level, according to Swift (141), in that their difficulties are concealed and rooted in different social perceptions rather than in resistance. In each case, these pupils will be seen as weaknesses of raw material, rather than as failures of the process. The school does not consider it has a need to comprehend such difficulties and the teacher does not see their failure as a threat to his role-conception.

The non-academic or non-selective school. This school provides secondary education for all those who do not succeed in the selection process. Since its conception, it has suffered from a lack of clarity so far as its goals were concerned. Theoretically, it had an opportunity to provide a true liberal education for pupils who were not to suffer from the constraints of an examination system. Exploration, discovery and experiment were to build upon the basic *plasticity* of the pupil who, although limited in his academic potentiality could still be helped to become a good worker, a good citizen and a good parent.

Unfortunately, the expectations of the participants in the process all differed from the official goals, and from each other. Parents and employers who were themselves educated within a traditional system could not adjust to criteria of personal development, social adjustment or potential ability, as methods of assessing educational achievement. They wanted some evidence to set against the formal evidence of the other side of the system, and they wanted an understandable method of comparing one unit of output with another.

Pupils who had been prepared for a system in which academic achievement was a criterion of progress, and in which performance was guided by the system, did not readily adapt to methods which did not seem to have an important end-result.

Headmasters could choose to try to emulate the organisation and achievements of the academic schools or to develop aims and methods which were unique to their own organisation. Their status within the profession was directly associated with the academic process and, therefore, most of them chose to try to prove that their organisation could be as successful in that process as the rest. One of the problems associated with change within the educational system is that innovation has to depend upon people who have been socialised for a considerable period within the institutional process. The policy of many education authorities in reserving selection for Headships to those whose seniority in experience is assured, is not conducive to the charismatic change which was required, if these new types of school were to succeed.

The staff were also in a position of role conflict. They had now to deal with raw material considered unsuitable for a process which they themselves had undergone and in which they had been successful. In most cases, their training had fitted them to be academic specialists with a major interest in a subject. The whole orientation of their profession was to emphasise the status and importance of such a concept of the role of the teacher. Yet they found themselves now in a process which minimised such aspects and stressed the importance of personal and social development of the pupils. This demanded qualities from the teacher for which their training had often not equipped them. Examinations, the criteria upon which they had depended to assess their results and the success of their efforts, were removed. Their training and experience made it difficult for them to conceive of other criteria. While they were in such a position of insecurity, the pressures from outside to develop conventional criteria were such that they succumbed with relief. The result was that much of the education became a pale imitation of that in the academic school and, as the Newsom Report stated, had become increasingly irrelevant for a large number of pupils.

It is an interesting point to reflect on whether this school need have failed, if the educational system and the teachers within it had been adequately prepared for the goals which were arbitrarily given to it. The same problem may still exist within the comprehensive school.

There was within the tri-partite system a third component – *the selective technical school* but we have not differentiated it from the academic component of our model.

3. Comprehensive education

The socially divisive and educationally dichotomous effects of the system we have described has led to the development of comprehensive education as a means of integrating the system.

The essence of our model is to emphasise the crucial importance to the success of such integration of the siting of comprehensive schools. If area schools are to be genuinely socially comprehensive, then they must be provided with a catchment area to include all the three 'ideal types' of primary school and residential area. To fail to do so would be to increase, rather than to decrease, social inequality within the system.

This raises the significant question as to whether educational policy might not be directed at the primary-school, or even nursery-school, level in order to eradicate the inequality before the secondary stage. The question also needs to be asked as to whether such inequality can be eradicated by the educational system, or whether it is not a more fundamental social issue.

It will also be evident that it is no solution to the problem of educational integration to combine the two 'ideal types' of secondary school within one unit.

If the larger comprehensive unit perpetuates the old dichotomy, then it is merely concealing the problem (126).

Neither can the goals of comprehensive education be achieved merely by organisation within the educational unit. A great deal of physical mixing can be accomplished by 'setting', rather than streaming, and by such devices as house systems which cut across age and educational differences, but social and educational integration may require a more positive approach. It may have to become a central activity of the organisation.

Social goals within the school may have to become as important as academic goals, and social performance may have to be rewarded equally with academic performance. Socialisation is dependent upon attitudes and performance within both formal and informal social situations and, therefore, the role expectations of many teachers may have to change to include a greater concern for personal and social relationships (51).

At present, curriculum development is largely seen as contributing to the greater efficiency of teachers in increasing the subject specialist aspect of their role. The use of auxiliaries and teaching aids can, however, be seen as releasing the teacher from involvement in the purveying of subject content and giving him more time to encourage pupil-orientated activity in which social relationships could be positively developed.

Large comprehensive units have an increasing number of pupils staying on until their late teens. They have a population of young people dependent upon the peer group for the development of values and attitudes (24).

4. *Youth culture*

Many complaints against present day society arise from the discomfort felt when living within the conflict caused by social change, when established institutions are being challenged and when embryonic institutions seem less adequate than those they replace.

At no point in society is this discomfort more strongly felt than in the relationship between adults and adolescents. If the adults expect from their adolescent children the patterns of behaviour which they themselves were taught, they may find that social conditions and needs have changed to the extent that adolescents find it necessary to choose between the social patterns of their parents, and the social patterns of contemporaries. This conflict or 'generation gap', added to the problem of role definition for the adolescent, tends to increase the importance of the 'peer group' of contemporaries as an aid to security and the formation of norms and attitudes.

The 'generation gap', plus the economic independence of many modern adolescents and the development of commercial interests to serve the emerging needs of the adolescent, gives rise to the development of a youth culture. This youth culture emphasises those areas of behaviour in which the adolescent can assert independence of adults and differences from them.

Adult-directed youth groups are one of the few remaining means available to adults who are trying to ensure the conformity of young people to adult standards. They are, therefore, attractive only to the adolescent ready to conform to adult standards, and to younger adolescents not yet ready for independence. There is evidence that traditional youth organisations find membership declining among the older adolescents and that, in any case, they attract only one in three. The adolescents less ready to conform to adult standards want to associate with their contemporaries independently of adult direction. Therefore, we observe the importance of meeting places, like coffee bars and beat clubs. Modern progressive youth-work tries to provide similar attractive environments for adolescents to associate with other young people (Albemarle (148).

The most important factor in the development of youth culture has been the increase in the last ten years of the earning power of the working teenager. In 1960, as Mark Abrams (1) pointed out, this group was commercially the most important in society, having the most uncommitted spending power, amounting at that time to £900 million pounds per year (this figure has since increased proportionately). Abrams showed that they dominated the market for bicycles, motor-cycles, record players, records, cinema entertainment, clothing, footwear and cosmetics. Probably the most prominent evidence of the commercial power of this group is the national, indeed international, importance of their 'idols'.

Working young people are part of the general movement in Britain to what Hoggart (45) calls 'short-winded reading' and are probably even more likely to confine their reading to comics, tabloids and magazines. Williams (103) has pointed to the low news content (about 10 per cent) of the popular newspapers and the indirect advertising in editorials of women's magazines, together with the total absence of current affairs in these magazines. In television itself there has again been some readiness to incorporate teenage standards and programmes, although teenagers do not watch as much as adults. In the film industry, there has been a development of the teenage romance as a subject for adult cinema.

While there is a reluctance to conform to adult requirements there is, nevertheless, a remarkable conformity to the demands of youth culture itself. An important aspect of this youth culture is its cross-cultural similarity, due to its particular receptiveness to the social and economic trends which are evident in most advanced societies. There is a similarity of behaviour between older school pupils, working teenagers and students (26).

Already the units of higher education within the educational system are learning that this inter-relationship between students within the educational system and the rest of the social system, can have wide repercussions within the educational system. It may be that schools have to be prepared for a similar effect.

5. *Higher education*

These units of higher education cannot assume that they are 'closed' systems insulated from the surrounding social system. A society which directs an increasing share of its financial resources towards the provision of education is concerned to learn how the money is spent. A technological society which depends for survival and progress upon the quality of the finished product of the educational process, is concerned to indicate what that product should be. As higher education recruits from a wider section of society, then the unit of higher education, like the schools, has to become aware of the variety of socialisation patterns and their effects.

Within the educational system, one of the outstanding problems is that suggested by our model in indicating the limited social recruitment of teachers and the requirement of those teachers to teach throughout the system. The educational system has to provide a professional socialisation for teachers, which will enable them to be sufficiently flexible to respond to a variety of different situations which demand different role performance. It also has to provide a process within the system to cope with on-going social change, so that role performance does not become institutionalised and resistant to innovation. This can be done partly by in-service courses but it also requires a close relationship between the system concerned with research and innovation and those concerned with educational practice in the field, so that gaps of communication and understanding are reduced (110).

SUMMARY

This chapter is concerned with the essential reciprocal relationship between education and society. The relevant aspects of the writings of certain classical sociologists are examined in order to illustrate the importance, to them, of this relationship. As in the case of the family, the educational system is seen to have changed considerably in structure and function as the social system has changed. The relationship between the educational system and each of the four sub-systems of society are examined in turn. The relationship between the community and education is examined in detail, by investigating a model of types of school as part of an input–output system. Areas of sociological knowledge are referred to as a clarification of this model.

NOTES

1. Timashaff (96), page 31.
2. Spencer, H. *First Principles* (Williams & Norgate 1910), page 321.
3. Spencer (92), page 61.
4. Spencer (92), page 127.
5. Martindale (64), page 88.
6. Durkheim (23), page 13.
7. Aron (2), page 86.

8. Consider all his numerous writings on the subject of which only two books have been translated into English thus far.

9. Durkheim (22), pages 16–17.

10. Ottaway (138), page 5.

11. Durkheim (22), page 71.

12. Durkheim (22), page 72.

13. Durkheim (22), page 117.

14. Ottaway (138), page 11.

15. Stevens (140) gives a complete list of Mead's work, including numerous articles on education.

16. Mead (66), page xiv.

17. Strauss (93), page 134.

18. Mead (66), page 265.

19. Mills, C. Wright and Gerth, Hans (Eds. and Trans.) *From Max Weber: Essays in Sociology* (Routledge & Kegan Paul 1948), page 74.

20. *Ibid.*, page 243.

21. *The Yearbook of Education* 1953 (Evans), page 4.

22. *The Yearbook of Education* 1954 (Evans), page 131.

23. Wilson (145), page 17.

24. *The World Yearbook of Education* 1967 (Evans), page 60.

25. Wilson (145), page 16.

26. *The World Yearbook of Education* 1967 (Evans), page 3.

27. Drucker, P. F. 'The Educational Revolution' in Halsey (40).

28. Vaizey, J. 'Should They be Written Off?' *The Sunday Times* (14th January 1968).

29. Burt, C. 'Ability and Income' *Brit. J. Educ. Psych.*, 13 (1943), pages 83–98.

30. This model is an elaboration of that described in an article by Ashley (114), and the chapter uses extensively the work of Jackson and Marsden (47), Wiseman (109), Musgrove and Taylor (137), Becker (117), Ashley, Cohen and Slatter (115), and the articles by Kob, J. 'The Role of the Teacher' in Halsey (40). Although the material is American, the book by R. E. Herriott and N. H. St. John, *Social Class and the Urban School* (Wiley (USA) 1966), has also been used for reference.

31. *CACE – Early Leaving Report* (HMSO 1954).

FURTHER READING

For an excellent summary of the research evidence relating to the effect of socio-economic status and environment on educational performance, see Wiseman (109), chapter 4.

Craft (18) contains further articles of direct relevance to the theme of this chapter.

A summary of research into the mass media, an important aspect of the relationship between the educational system and society not dealt with in this book, can be found in Halloran (39).

The article by Wilson (145) illustrates the close inter-relationship between education and society in so far as it has an impact on the teacher.

A companion volume in this series, Musgrave (79), extends the historical analysis and describes school organisation.

5 The Teaching-Learning Process in the School and Classroom

Some factors which have already been discussed as relationships between the educational system and the social system, or between school and community, need to be looked at again within the school itself. The sociology of the school is a subject in itself (79) but we must be satisfied with proposing a model to analyse interaction within the school and then looking closely at the primary unit in the school, namely, the classroom group.

A MODEL FOR THE ANALYSIS OF THE TEACHING–LEARNING PROCESS

This model (Figure 6) is based upon a number of sources. Using the social system model of Parsons (see chapter 2) and Lessnoff (132), it incorporates the different analysis of a number of other

Figure 6 Model of Teaching–Learning Process in the School

MEANS	ENDS
Adaptive	Goal attainment
custodial	elementary
EXTERNAL academic	preparatory
missionary or	developmental
crusading	
Pattern maintenance and	Integrative
tension management	coercive
teacher oriented	utilitarian
INTERNAL subject or task	normative
oriented	
learner oriented	

writers: namely, the coercive, utilitarian and normative used by Etzioni (27); the missionary and crusading division referred to by Floud[1]; elementary, preparatory and developmental after Blyth[2]; and the teacher, learner and subject-centred emphases mentioned by Withall (147). It is the essence of our model that each of these other writers was differentiating between parts of the total system, whereas it is possible to relate these observed differences to each other within that system.

Before considering the model in detail it must again be emphasised, following the social system approach, that those functions directed towards the external environment, and those directed towards its internal arrangement, exercise reciprocal controls and influences. Similarly, the ends of the system and the means used to achieve them are reciprocally related.

It will be seen that three school types can be derived from the model by tracing the inter-cell relationships as follows:

	pattern maintenance and tension management	integrative	goal achievement	adaptive
Type 1	teacher oriented	coercive	elementary	custodial
Type 2	subject oriented	utilitarian	preparatory	academic
Type 3	learner oriented	normative	developmental	missionary/ crusading

Again, it should be pointed out that no school is likely to fit completely within these clearly differentiated categories. For instance, even the most 'cramming' conscious school contains classes and teachers exhibiting different degrees of subject-centredness. Such a school with a predominant orientation will occasionally relax and allow other orientations to emerge. Nevertheless, we feel that it may be useful to isolate the differences by this model.

Type 1

One of the major problems facing any social system, large or small, complex or simple, is that of maintaining its pattern or structure. This does not preclude the possibility of changes occurring in that structure, but changes, when they occur, are usually based on the existing structure. Thus, any social system must have processes of socialisation whereby the cultural patterns of the system come to be incorporated into the personalities of its members (see chapter 3).

In this first type of school, the socialisation or learning process is completely centred on the teacher as a representative of the system. The system is all-important and the participant must conform to the system. To participate in the system is considered sufficient in itself. There is no selection and all are accepted. The teacher is seen as embodying all the virtues of the system which require to be inculcated. The authority which the system gives to the position of teacher emphasises the importance of the example given by the teacher. His training emphasises moral virtues and exemplary behaviour.

To facilitate this process, there must be control through a distribution of rewards and punishments. In this organisation control is based on coercion. Compliance is forced upon the members and failure to comply incurs punishment which may be physical or restrictive (e.g. detention, exclusion from favourite activities), or abusive (e.g. insults, sarcasm).

The adaptive function involves coming to terms with the external situation and environment and deciding appropriate techniques for achieving the desired ends. For this reason, we have described the adaptive function of this first type as *custodial*, in that it sees its purpose or goal as being very limited or elementary. This is a term used by Blyth to describe those primary schools (it is used here as being applicable to any school) in which the emphasis is upon an 'enforced conformity to minimal rules and standards' and upon punishment rather than reward. This was the limited aim of elementary education during the nineteenth century, namely, to turn out obedient and respectful pupils who would not challenge the *status quo*. The method of teaching in such schools was largely by rote and drill – and even today it is not unknown for such a didactic approach to predominate.

Type 2

In this school the system, as such, becomes less important than the body of knowledge which is to be transmitted to the pupils.

The pupils are expected to accept the body of knowledge because of its relevance and usefulness. Therefore, selection is introduced to ensure that the pupils are capable of dealing with the body of knowledge. The teacher receives his authority in the process from the knowledge he possesses and from the qualifications he holds. His training emphasises the psychological as a means of assessing the capacity of his pupils to understand his subject.

In this school, the control rests on the utilitarian nature of the education. Pupils can be expected to 'work hard' in order to achieve recognition within the process, through passing examinations, receiving certificates and degrees. Pupils are more committed to the system than in the previous coercive example, but their commitment is calculative in that education is seen as a means to an end, rather than an end in itself.

We use Blyth's term 'preparatory' to describe the goal achievement function of this type of school. His description of the preparatory tradition, as seeing pupils as 'competing individuals' and of its emphasis on a 'rather predetermined pattern of norms, coloured by the presumed requirements of acculturation', also appears to tie in with Turner's view of the British educational system as a sponsored system.[3] This achievement of the goal of preparation (preparation for successive stages within the educational process and, ultimately, preparation for positions demanding qualifications and acceptable behaviour) is brought about by stressing the academic aspect of education. Thus, the degree of success of the adaptive and goal achievement functions, each oriented to the environment external to the educational system, can be seen by outsiders by permitting objective standards to be applied – in this case, the figures relating to examination successes.

Type 3

In the third school, the learning process itself is all-important. This process is focused upon the development of the pupil. The teacher is involved in the process as a facilitator of the development of the pupil. As such, he becomes, as Etzioni suggests, more concerned with expressive activities rather than instrumental activities. He is required to understand his pupils as social beings and to take account of their social context. His training needs to take increasing account of the sociological, as well as the psychological factors in training. The counselling and social work aspects of the role are emphasised in a school which is essentially a 'caring' institution. The problem of ensuring control relies heavily upon engaging the commitment and motivation of the pupils, by involving them in the process of establishing an 'evolving democratic community'.

This process of obtaining their commitment concerns itself with what Etzioni has called 'the normative approach' to the problem of securing internal control and integration. He stresses the symbolic element of the normative approach as opposed to the more tangible elements within the coercive and utilitarian methods. These symbolic elements he divides into three categories. 'Normative' control is exercised directly by the teacher to control the pupils, as when he gives them a pep-talk on such issues as not letting the school down by engaging in unruly behaviour at a football match. 'Normative-social' power is used indirectly as, for example, when a teacher appeals to the peer-group of a pupil to exercise control over him. An illustration of this may be the situation where a class or a group is punished collectively (this brings in an element of coercion), because no one has admitted to committing a misdemeanour, and is then told that it can deal later with the offender in an informal manner. The third category is 'social' control, whereby the peers directly exercise control over one another. Etzioni argues that this, as such, is not a form of organisational power and is, therefore, not discussed. But it cannot be validly left out of any consideration of the school situation, for there are times when a peer-group can, and does, exercise powerful control over its members. This control may, perhaps, be exercised in an extremely anti-school direction and so directly influence the behaviour of an individual within the school. Nevertheless, Etzioni suggests that 'organisations which rely heavily on normative power are the most successful in terms of their socialisation achievements. Modern schools are a prime example.'[4] This approach requires that the pupils actively participate in the evolution of norms within the school.

The developmental goal seeks to adjust the 'process of socialisation to the children's growing capacities for social and moral behaviour and with promoting children's experience of a wide range of social roles'.[5] But, in comparison with the more clearly defined objectives of the utilitarian approach, this means that success and failure is less clear-cut and both from the teachers' point of view and that of outsiders, this allows uncertainty and subjectivity to replace certainty and objectivity.

To achieve this, we use Floud's idea that teachers be missionaries in the slums or near slums and crusaders in the suburbs. She suggests that the idea of the teacher–missionary be more appropriately replaced by that of the teacher–social worker. The complementary aspect of the role of teacher 'dedicated to the war against mediocrity and to the search for excellence' is that of the crusader in the less deprived areas.[6]

FURTHER IMPLICATIONS OF THE MODEL

In chapter 4 we illustrated the complex inter-relationships between the educational system and the sub-systems within society. The model presented in the previous section outlines the effects of those relationships within the school.

The school can choose as an adaptive function either to adjust to 'inflexible reality' or 'actively transform the environment'.[7] If the school follows the first possibility, then it may be described as acting mainly as an agent of social continuity, whereas in following the second possibility, it is acting as an agent of social change.

Of the three types of learning-teaching process, it appears that the first two are mainly concerned with adjusting to inflexible reality. This is achieved by techniques, such as enforcing conformity and obedience, emphasising the practical value of education in securing the 'better' jobs after leaving school, stressing the value of competition and establishing procedures of streaming and selection.

The third type, in contrast, is more concerned with attempting to emphasise changes and 'diversity rather than the One Right Way'.[8] It can be argued that the 1944 Education Act and, perhaps even more so the recent moves to make secondary education comprehensive, are attempts to modify the social structure. The techniques employed by the schools include the abolition of streaming and selection, the decline in the use of punishment with a corresponding increase in the use of reward for effort and not merely for success, and the involvement of the pupils in establishing the norms within the school and classroom.

Implicit in the model is the assumption that the values and aims of the teachers are, at the very least, in close accord with those embodied in the school organisation. This, as we suggested in chapter 4, is not always so, but space prevents discussion of the role stresses and conflicts pertaining to the position of teacher.[9] The effects of the attitudes and methods adopted by teachers should also be studied in other work.[10]

One might not go as far as Floud in stating that a child's educability 'depends *as much* on the assumptions, values and aims personified in the teacher and embodied in the school organisation into which he is supposed to *assimilate himself as on those* he brings with him from his home'.[11] But it is the interaction of these attitudes, values and aims which shapes the educational process.

As examples, we examine briefly two of these factors which pupils bring into the school situation, namely, language and motivation, which are among the most significant in influencing the pattern of the teaching–learning process.

Language

The importance of language in the socialisation process is stressed by many writers in statements, such as, 'Language is probably the greatest force of socialisation – significant social intercourse is hardly possible without language'[12] and 'communicative contact is the core of socialisation' (19). Lawton (55) suggests that attempts to bring about structural changes in society, by such moves as the introduction of comprehensive secondary education, will have only limited success unless efforts are made also to 'provide opportunities for the extension of linguistic facility within educational institutions'.

Attention will be focused upon speech, which normally takes precedence over other kinds of communicative symbolism, viz. writing (substitutive) and gestures (supplementary) and upon the work of Bernstein in this field (118, 119, 120).

In his analysis of the social origins of different patterns of language in Britain, Bernstein describes two 'codes' with noticeably different characteristics and consequences. These are the *elaborated code*, in which the meaning is 'explicit and finely differentiated' and which is more typically a middle-class pattern, and the *restricted code* which is typically lower working class, with the meaning 'implicit and crudely differentiated'.

Some of the characteristics of the restricted code (those of the elaborated code are much the opposite) are short and often incomplete sentences with few adverbs or adjectives, but frequent use of idiomatic phrases, sentences often ending with questioning phrases such as 'wouldn't it' or 'you know' (in contrast, the elaborated code users more frequently use the phrase 'I think'). The extensive use of idiom may cause some to confuse the vigour and colour of the restricted code with a fluency and range of possibilities it does not possess.

At first sight, it may appear that Bernstein is merely showing the correlation between social class and the code of speech. Actually, however, he is illustrating the connection between speech and the nature of the social relationships to be found in different groupings in our society. Thus, the restricted code is generated where there is a strong sense of similarity and solidarity among the people, allegedly a characteristic of working-class areas. There is, therefore, little need for verbal explanation by an individual because of these similarities. This reduces the need for verbal elaboration which, in turn, reduces the need for adjectives and develops a limited interest in abstract concepts with an associated lack of abstract terms.

The elaborated code is generated among those who adopt a rather more individualistic outlook upon life, allegedly a characteristic of the middle-class. This emphasis upon difference rather than upon similarity, necessitates verbal elaboration – this is reinforced by the willingness of middle-class parents to attempt rational explanations in response to the child's questions. And so the child from such an environment grows up accepting explicit and finely differentiated verbalisation.

Bernstein emphasises that these differences in language patterns are not necessarily generated by differences in intelligence, but rather by differences in social relationships to be found in different environments. Nevertheless, there is a tendency for those children who are elaborated code users to score more highly in intelligence tests, particularly in those tests which necessitate some verbal ability.

Other consequences are that children from lower working-class homes experience difficulty in learning to read and in comprehending relationships between classes of objects. While they may be able to cope with the demands of mechanical arithmetic, they often have difficulty coping with 'problems' – to them 'sums with words'. They may, therefore, do fairly well in the early stages of their primary education, but not so well in the later stages and in the secondary school when a move from concrete to abstract operations is involved. This, coupled with a short-term span of attention, may well lead to apathy or unruliness as a defence against the demands of the school.

In his research intended to duplicate and extend Bernstein's work, Lawton (55) found that the middle-class/working-class difference in the use of elaborated and restricted codes applies to written work as well as to speech. In group discussions his findings were 'remarkably similar' to those of Bernstein. In individual interviews his results were generally in agreement with Bernstein's theory but, interestingly, although working-class pupils experienced difficulty in switching to elaborated code usage, their speech did not break down completely as might have been expected.

Motivation

The link between language and motivation has been stressed by Josephine Klein (53) in her analysis of sub-cultural characteristics to be found in Britain. She suggests that there are four areas in which the links between patterns of behaviour and of speech can be seen: in the ability to make generalisations from the concrete actual situation; in the ability to see the world as an ordered universe in which rational and ordered behaviour is rewarded; in the ability to exercise self-control and to plan for the future. The degree of verbal elaboration will influence perception of factors relating to the general, the abstract and the future. Hence, 'verbal skills have motivational as well as cognitive implications' because they are necessary to 'create a conception of an orderly universe in which rationally considered action is more likely to be rewarded than impulsive behaviour'.

This concept of the differences between long-term goals and achieving more immediate satisfaction rests largely upon the work of McClelland (61). He claims that high achievement motivation is more likely to be found in those sub-cultures and families where there is an emphasis on individual development. This led to work emphasising the fact that higher achievement motivation is more characteristic of middle-class than working-class families. In terms of the more specific academic achievement motivation, it is put thus:

. . . the children who do the best work, are easiest to control and stimulate, make the best prefects, stay at school longest, take part in the extra-curricular activities, finish school with the best qualifications and references and get into the best jobs, tend to come from the middle class (142).

THE CLASSROOM GROUP

In this section, we will examine the classroom situation in the light of knowledge gained through the study of groups in the past two-and-a-half decades. The study of the changes in the structure and function of small groups has come to be known as GROUP DYNAMICS. This area gained impetus during the war, when a number of studies of small-group behaviour were undertaken. In its development, it has been influenced by psychologists and sociologists, drawing its highly sophisticated experimental techniques from the former and its dominant theoretical framework from the latter. The potential of group dynamics in education was realised in the 1940s (5), but little work was done until the past decade. Neal Gross, in his review of the work in this area, remarks on the fact that sociologists have ignored the 'teacher–pupil relationship' and that, although there has been much work on small groups in the laboratory, 'there have been few efforts to replicate these studies in the small-group settings of the classroom'.[13] In many respects the situation is much the same a decade later, and insufficient work is being done in an area which is ideally suited for small-group research, the results of which could be fruitful for the sociologist and valuable for the teacher and educator.

Some characteristics of classroom groups

In chapter 2, we briefly outlined what we understood by the concept group and discussed some of the different ways of classifying groups. In the light of that discussion, we propose to examine the classroom group and determine what are its main characteristics. We must agree with Bany and Johnson (5) when they suggest that the classroom group is one of the most important groups in the life of the child. It is a group in which many of his needs are met and much of his learning occurs. It is, therefore, important from a teacher's point of view to know more about this group.

The classroom group can, but need not always be, a primary group. If we look at the classroom situation at the start of a new academic year, we see that, initially, it is an aggregate within a large formal organisation, the school. The school, it would seem, is what we have called a secondary group. The classroom group fulfils all the physical characteristics of Cooley's primary group, that is, the members are in face-to-face interaction; there is usually a small number of participants and it exists for a relatively long time. Thus, after some time, we can at least expect primary group relationships to emerge between the children in the class, in all probability a number of primary groups will come into being. However, if we include the teacher in the classroom group, and if we are to consider the classroom group as a teaching–learning situation, we must include the teacher; the class no longer forms a complete primary group. It still retains all the physical characteristics of the primary group described above, but the teacher symbolizes the secondary group, the school as a whole. The teacher brings to the classroom the formal authority of the school organisation, which alters the nature of the situation, particularly the relational characteristics.

We may examine these relational characteristics in the classroom by seeing whether they are predominantly those which we normally find in a primary group or a secondary one. In Davis (19) we find a convenient breakdown of what he calls the social characteristics of the two types of groups; we will use these but refer to them as relational characteristics.

For a classroom group to be a primary one, it would need to manifest the following relational characteristics:

1. There would have to be a mutual identification of ends and goals between the participants, this is the case in most instances between the children, but need not be so as far as the teacher is concerned. The teacher is there to teach – he might view his work merely as a job, a means of income. (In Davis' terms there is a 'disparity of ends' between the teacher and the pupil, thus making it more of a secondary-type relationship.)

2. For the relationship to be of the primary-group type, the participants are expected to value the relation and persons intrinsically. By this is meant that members regard the relationships and others in the group as ends in themselves, and not as means to an end (extrinsically), as they would in a secondary group. Again, it can be seen that the children in the class tend to regard each other as friends and thus have an intrinsic regard for each other and the relationship, whereas the teacher is more likely to consider the children extrinsically, particularly in secondary schools.

3. Members of a primary group usually have inclusive knowledge about each other (as one finds in a family: the parent knows much about the child). The teacher's knowledge of the child is, however, specialised and limited, being more concerned with the child's behaviour and personal history insofar as it relates to the task at hand. If we regard the teacher's role as being child-centred, of the counsellor type concerned with the whole person, it veers in the direction of the primary-type relationship; whereas, if we regard it as subject-centred, concerned with the task and only a limited area of the person, it veers in the direction of the secondary-type relationship.

4. Controls in the primary group are informal and there is a feeling of freedom and spontaneity among the participants, whereas in the secondary the controls tend to be formal and the participants are aware of external constraints on their behaviour. Again, in the classroom we find both situations; the children in their interactions among themselves tend to exercise informal controls and be spontaneous, but once we include the teacher we note that he exercises formal control, the authority of the Head or educational board is vested in him, this leads to external constraints being imposed both on his behaviour and the children's.

In many instances, teachers will manage to establish primary-group type relations with the children, but the point is that the threat of formal sanctions and external constraints are always there. It would seem, therefore, that the classroom group contains both characteristics of a primary and a secondary group at one and the same time. It consists of a number of primary groups among the children, and of a secondary group if we include the teacher. The classroom, which has all the physical characteristics of a primary group, has primary relations among its pupils, but secondary between the pupils and the teacher. We consider that this is a tension-producing situation, partly accounting for Willard Waller's suggestion that the teacher–pupil relationship is one of dominance and subordination and continual conflict.

Teacher and pupil confronted each other in the school with an original conflict of desires . . . The teacher represent the adult group, ever the enemy of the spontaneous life of groups of children.[14]

In our view, it is not so much that the teacher represents the adult world but the secondary group which turns him into the 'enemy' of the children's groups, the primary groups. This is obviously a structural conflict, one which is built into our present educational system, and as Waller further suggests – that no matter what the teacher does to reduce the conflict it will still remain. This distinction of group membership and loyalty on the part of teachers and pupils will colour all the relations they have. This type of distinction is, of course, not unique to the classroom group, but will be found in the army, industry or any situation where small groups of people interact within the framework of a larger group.

Analysing the classroom group in terms of the type of relationship that exists in it is important in that it highlights these problems of conflict, as well as suggesting other possible sources of difficulty in the pupil's adjustment to the school situation. For example, a child entering school for the first time is moving not only from the physical environment of the home to the school, but into a new social environment as well. The child has to make a jump from having only experienced relationships inside a primary group, the family, to a new set of relationships inside a secondary group, the school. This relational shift can be very difficult and requires careful handling. The movement from the primary school to the secondary contains a similar change in relationships, although they might not be as marked. If we consider Davis' social characteristics, we can see that the child has to adjust to a new assessment of himself, for example, to move from a world where he has been treated informally, spontaneously, as an end in himself and where his parents have inclusive knowledge about him, to one which is virtually the opposite. Admittedly, many of our primary schools are well aware of this problem and attempt to make the shift easy for the child, but this simply forestalls the problem, as he must face this relational shift when he enters secondary school.

We have discussed the dichotomous nature of the classroom group with reference to the distinction between primary and secondary groups. We could just as well see this division reflected in another distinction, between formal and informal. Formally, the classroom group is a work or task group and informally, for the pupils, it is a friendship group. As a formal work group, it has much in common with other work groups, but also some important distinctions. Some of the following features are regarded by Bany and Johnson (5) as being specific to the classroom group.

1. A classroom group is regarded as unique because its purpose is to 'produce changes in the group members themselves'. Most industrial work-groups are producing changes in some object and are not consciously concerned with changes among themselves.
2. The goals of the classroom group are prescribed by people external to it, this is similar to most other work-groups found in industry.
3. The members of a classroom group may be regarded as forming a PEER GROUP, that is, they are all contemporaries usually the same age, and tend to have similar needs and interests. In a factory work-group it is unusual to have such a high degree of homogeneity among the members.
4. Unlike most other groups the members of a classroom group have to be there. Membership is compulsory and pupils have no choice in deciding whether they wish to attend, even the parents have limited rights in this respect. In industrial work-groups attendance is voluntary, and members need not attend, the sanctions are economic and not legal as in the school.

5. Classroom groups are usually part of a larger secondary-group, most work-groups follow the same pattern.
6. The leadership pattern in the classroom is not unlike that in other formal groups. One important distinction between the two is that the members of the classroom have no institutionalised means of voicing grievances and bargaining for better work conditions and hours; in a sense they are totally defranchised in their work situation and without adequate representation. Although recent events both here and abroad suggest that students and pupils are beginning to organise and make demands on the system, the present essentially authoritarian school pattern is likely to remain for some time.

Leadership in the classroom group

Leadership is an important aspect of the classroom situation and is, after all, from the teacher's point of view an aspect of his role, some might go so far as to say it *is* the teacher's role. In our examination of leadership in the classroom, we are not concerned with the personality factors which go to make up a leader, nor with any leader that emerges among the pupils, but with the role of the teacher as a leader. The teacher is a leader in the classroom in so far as he influences and controls the thoughts and behaviour of his pupils and sets the tone of the interaction patterns in the classroom. This he can do because of the position he occupies in the structure and the power and authority he gains by virtue of being a member of the organisational 'elite'. Thelen has described the teacher as having seven models of leadership which he uses in the classroom. For example, the conventional 'boss-employee' image – the teacher has power and status and can reward and punish the child; the 'Socratic discussion' group, here the image is of a wise old philosopher using the dialectic method to clarify concepts; or another which he calls the 'town meeting', which is the image of a small group of townspeople meeting to discuss problems which confront them.[15] These models are of interest to the teacher because they may help to clarify his own conception of his role.

A study of leadership which has a different approach, and is of equal importance to teachers, is one which considers the effects of different leadership styles on the children. A classical study of

I

this type was conducted by one of the pioneers of group dynamics, Kurt Lewin; together with two other researchers he studied leader behaviour and the reaction of the followers in different social climates.[16]

The three different social climates which the researchers succeeded in creating were ones in which, in each case, the leader behaviour was either 'democratic', 'authoritarian' or 'laissez-faire'. Four clubs of ten-year-old boys were formed, each club consisting of five members. The boys were matched on a number of characteristics in an effort to make the groups as much like each other as possible. Four adults were instructed in how to play the role of 'democratic', 'authoritarian' and 'laissez-faire' leaders, and were rotated among the four groups. The result was that each adult played each leadership style in each of the four groups. The purpose of this rather complicated procedure was to minimize the effect of the individual leader's personality on the group, and allow the researchers to explain differences in the groups' responses to the leaders' behaviour by the particular leadership style experienced in that group. An interesting aspect of the study was the definition of the different leadership roles in behavioural terms. Thus, the *authoritarian* leader was directive, he determined all policies, techniques and activities of the group. He assigned working companions and dictated the particular work that was to be done. In his criticisms he was personal and remained aloof from the group except when demonstrating what was the next process. In marked contrast to this, in the *democratic* leader style, the leader encouraged discussion, all policies were determined by group discussion and decision. He gave technical advice, but tried to offer alternatives so that the boys could have a choice, allowed the children to work with whom they wished and do very much as they pleased. In his praise or criticism, the leader remained objective and 'fact-minded' and tried to be a 'regular' member of the group. In contrast with the two styles, the *laissez-faire* leader was less active. He allowed complete freedom in policies and techniques and was only prepared to participate when directly asked. He made no attempt to praise or criticise the group's work, and remained outside the group, but not aloof. The actual setting out in behavioural terms of what is meant by concepts we commonly use in a hazy political manner, is a useful approach to the study of leadership. Furthermore, it is useful for teachers as it sets out explicitly in behavioural terms what is meant by authoritarian, democratic and *laissez-faire* leadership styles.

The groups' responses to these different styles of leadership were observed in detail and recorded. It was found that the group responded in definite patterns to the different leadership styles. The *authoritarian* style resulted in two reactions: in one case a passive response and in the other an aggressive one. In the 'aggressive autocracy' there was a high amount of hostile behaviour, but together with the 'apathetic autocracy', they both shared a marked need for dependence on the leader. When there was a change of leadership from authoritarian to democratic or *laissez-faire*, they showed a big increase in the amount of horse-play between the members. The observers concluded that in the apathetic group this reflected latent feelings of hostility. There was evidence to suggest that the democratic and *laissez-faire* responses were not the same. In the latter, there was less work done and of a poorer quality, and in an interview the boys expressed preference for their democratic leader. Although the quantity of work done in the autocracy was greater than the democracy, work motivation in the latter was higher and there was more originality among the boys. The democratic group showed more 'group-mindedness' and more friendliness.

These studies are not directly concerned with the classroom situation, but their relevance to teachers are reasonably obvious, in so far as they suggest that the teacher by adopting a particular style of leadership in the classroom will, in all probability, get very different responses from his pupils. These different responses are likely to have an effect on the children's motivation to learn, and the quality of the children's work, plus their general feeling of well-being as a member of the class.

These different styles of leadership when applied to the class-room group have been called 'teacher-centred' and 'learner-centred'. Using what can only be described as a modification of the Lewin dichotomy of autocratic/democratic leadership styles, attempts have been made to determine how the teacher's role performance in the classroom can be classified (146). Techniques

for rating and observing the teacher's behaviour in the classroom
have been developed; rating has been found to be different for
people in different roles in the teacher's role set.[17] This is only to
be expected and does not entirely invalidate the findings of people
using this technique, as to seek for objective assessment of the
teacher's role performance, without reference to the people he is
interacting with, seems void of any meaning. However, observers
brought into the classroom can provide some objectivity but this
is a particularly difficult and sensitive area for research and might
account for the small number of studies. R. Anderson found,
after reviewing a number of studies using the autocratic/demo-
cratic dichotomy, that this appeared to be an over-simplification
of what actually went on in the classroom. A teacher was not one
or the other – there could be different shades of each style – and
it might, in fact, be invalid to suggest that the teacher-centred or
authoritarian role is always necessarily impersonal and hostile. It
would be possible for a teacher to remain an authoritarian and, at
the same time, have warm personal relations with the pupils; this,
it would seem, would depend very much on the general belief
current in the society as a whole. In a society like ours which
regards itself as democratic, authoritarian patterns might lead to
hostility. The research in this area seems to reflect these problems
and is inconclusive, some researchers reporting that 'learner-
centred' classes produce more learning; others, that 'teacher-
centred' ones do so (42). It would seem that the overall tendency
is to suggest that the 'learner-centred' or 'group-centred' approach
is more concerned with the pupils' well-being, and the 'teacher-
centred' with the subjects being studied. It is probably necessary
for the teacher to be able to adopt either style, depending on the
needs of the pupils and the total situation in which interaction is
taking place.

Methods of acquiring information about the classroom group

There are a number of different techniques which may be used
to observe a classroom-group interacting. The most important
aspect of these is the framework used. The observer cannot see
and record everything, therefore, he must select certain activities
as being relevant to the problem he is handling. Most observers

will develop their own categories for observation; this can be difficult, as to be relevant and theoretically consistent is not always an easy task. A highly elaborate and detailed technique has been developed by Bales (3) for observing problem-solving activities in groups. 'Interaction process analysis', as Bales calls his system of observation, obtains information about the 'social–emotional' and 'task areas' within a group. In a problem-solving situation members of a group are interacting with each other, they have feelings about each other as well as the task. After much work, Bales has arrived at six categories dealing with the 'social–emotional areas', the affective aspects of the situation, and six dealing with 'task areas', the instrumental aspects of the situation. Although this is an interesting technique, it is far too complicated for most observers and can only provide the teacher with guide-lines as to what may be relevant in the classroom work-group.

A far easier technique for obtaining information about groups, particularly classroom primary groups, is that of SOCIOMETRY. This is a method of determining interpersonal relations in a group. It was developed by Moreno (76) in Austria and later in America; he inspired a number of followers who have continued and expanded his work in this field. One of these fellow workers, Helen H. Jennings, has described sociometry

. . . as a means of presenting simply and graphically the entire structure of relations existing at a given time among members of a given group. The major lines of communication, or the pattern of attraction and rejection in its full scope, are made readily comprehensive at a glance.[18]

It is doubtful whether sociometry describes the 'entire structure' of a group as claimed by this definition, but it certainly does reveal the patterns of attraction and rejection in a small group. It is this very aspect that makes it so suitable for studying primary groups, which are groups containing a high degree of emotional content.

The sociometric questionnaire consists of asking each child to specify, privately, whom he would like or not like to sit next to, associate with, work with, or partner in any other appropriate activity. Once this information is obtained, it is organised into a choice-matrix, by listing all the names of the pupils in the class on a vertical axis and repeating them in the same order on a horizontal axis. The choices are then related to each other, thus obtaining a choice-matrix for that class. This information can be presented in diagrammatic form (see figure 7), that is, each member of the class is located in a structure consisting of lines of attraction or rejection.

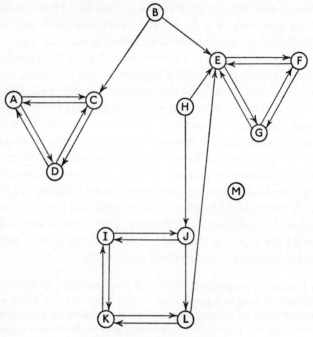

Figure 7   Example of a Sociogram

The sociogram shows only positive choices in a small group. Each line represents a choice, the arrow indicates the direction. Thus, at a glance, we can see that the child represented by the letter E has received the most choices and would be known as a STAR. Children such as B and H who make choices but are not chosen in turn by anyone are called NEGLECTEES. In some instances, a child makes no choices himself and is not chosen by any member of the class; he is known as an ISOLATE. A child who is rejected by other members of the class is known as a REJECTEE.

This kind of information can be valuable to the teacher; in some cases it can confirm his assessments arrived at by observation, or show him how out-of-touch he might be with the pupils' assessments of each other. It allows him the opportunity to do something about the isolates and rejectees, if he feels this to be necessary.

Sociometry has been used in a large number of studies in the classroom situation, many of which have been conducted in Britain (29). A summary of some of the findings which frequently occur among children has been made by Blyth (122). He notes that the intensity of the sex cleavage is always high in pre-adolescence, sometimes almost complete. When a child is a star, the tendency is for him to accumulate more choices. Negative choices, that is rejections, have a higher intensity than positive ones and tend to be more stable. This type of information can be useful for teachers, particularly if they see their role as child-centred or as containing an element of counselling.

A model of the classroom group

It is in the classroom group that most of the actual work of the school gets done. However, the trend today is to some extent away from the classroom as the only teaching–learning situation. The introduction of new subjects, containing less academic content, and the increasing emphasis on practical content will tend to take the teaching–learning situation outside of the classroom. A similar move in this direction can be found in the attempt to break down the idea of a school as a series of boxes, and to mix classes together under a group of teachers. Both these trends suggest a search for more effective and relevant methods of teaching and learning. Nevertheless, it remains true to say that, irrespective of the situation, most of the teaching and learning done today takes place in a group situation, usually the classroom group.

Parsons, in his article on the school class as a social system has suggested that the class has two important functions.[19] First, the school class can be treated as an 'agency of socialisation'. This means that the class is the means through which the members of our society are taught to want and be able to perform adequate roles in the system. As we have already noted (see chapter 3), the school class is not the only agency of socialisation, the family and peer-group perform this function initially. The second important function of the class is as an 'agency of manpower allocation'. In this role, the school class performs the function of selecting people for certain roles in the society. The achievement of the pupils at every level of the school system, particularly the later levels, will affect their employment prospects. Parsons' study of the school class as a social system, although an interesting and original contribution, deals primarily with the external features; in this section, however, we are more concerned with the internal features of the classroom group.

The work of Getzels and Thelen, based on Parsons, provides us with a model which is mainly concerned with these features. They consider the classroom group as a unique social system. Although many features of the classroom group can be found in other groups, its unique quality lies 'in the peculiar configuration of the specific characteristics'.[20] They see the main goal of the classroom group as that of learning. A distinctive feature is that it is planned learning, and a goal which is consciously held and set by people external to the class.

In the same way that any unit can be analysed as a system, so the model which they develop is applicable to school or class irrespective of the size. They conceive of the social system as containing two conceptually distinct and independent phenomena, which influence each other. These are socio-cultural phenomena, which they call NOMOTHETIC, and bio-psychological, which they call IDEOGRAPHIC. The nomothetic dimension of behaviour, sometimes referred to as the normative dimension, consists of the following major elements: institutions, roles and expectations. The ideographic dimension, or personal dimension, consists of the following elements: need-dispositions (needs of the individual), personalities and individuals. The distinction between the two dimensions can be regarded as being much the same as that between sociological factors and psychological factors. The distinction between the biological and anthropological (cultural) dimensions can easily be seen in their model reproduced in Figure 8.

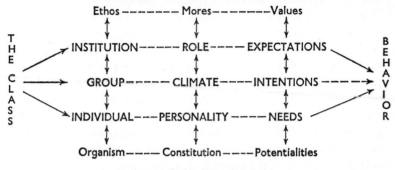

Figure 8   Model of the Classroom Group as a Unique
Social System[21]

Thus, if we examine the model, we see that the cultural dimension consists of the ethos, mores and values of the system. The institutionalised expectations of roles are related to the values and mores of the culture in which they exist. Thus, we would only expect pupils to play certain roles in particular cultures. In most capitalist societies the pupil is not expected to be concerned with politics, whereas in communist societies this is seen as part of his classroom learning. The strongly held ethic of achievement in most industrial societies, particularly in the USA, strongly influences all aspects of the pupil's role and the expectations of all concerned with his education.

In much the same way, we can see the biological organism with a particular constitution and potentialities influencing the psychological characteristics. The authors suggest that in working out the balance between these two dimensions, the socio-cultural and bio-psychological, the group develops a climate or atmosphere, which can be analysed as the intentions of the group.

The model is used to analyse conflict in the classroom, which is always a problem teachers have to face. Getzels and Thelen suggest that conflict is likely to arise in a number of areas. For example, between 'cultural values outside the classroom and the institutional expectations within the classroom'.[22] They suggest that our culture is tending to prize hedonistic values which are in conflict with the achievement goals of the classroom. There are other ways in which conflict might arise in a system. For example, between role expectations and personality dispositions.

On the basis of the model, they identify three types of teaching styles. First, the nomothetic style, which emphasises the institutionalised role requirement of the system over and above the personality of the individual. In this teaching style, education is seen as 'the handing down of what is known to those who do not yet know'.[23] Secondly, we have the ideographic style, which emphasises the personality of the individual over and above the role expectations of the institution. In this approach, education is defined as 'helping the person know what he wants to know'.[24] The third style they call the transactional, which is intermediate between the other two. In this style, the teacher is required to make intelligent use of the other two styles as the situation demands. The important element in it, however, is the awareness of the role the group plays in the classroom as a mediator between the institution and the individual, or as a means of controlling or imposing institutional norms on the individual.

This model's value is in the fact that it allows us to think systematically about a complex process. It also provides us with descriptions of three different roles of the teacher in the classroom group, which emerge out of the very structure and process of this group. Westwood (144) has suggested that the model has limitations, particularly in that, as it tends to be a static view of the classroom, it fails to take account of the way the roles might change. Nevertheless, although the model has its weaknesses it provides a good basis for further research – particularly in the role of the teacher. In some respects, it reflects the general state of the sociology of education, which has many underdeveloped areas requiring further research.

SUMMARY

In this chapter some of the factors which were investigated as manifesting the relationship between the educational system and the wider social system, and particularly the community, are looked at again in a different way. We narrow our perspective to the school, as the system, and concern ourselves with the interaction within the school itself. This is such an important aspect of the sociology of education as to be a subject in itself (79). We propose a model for the analysis of interaction in the school, and discuss some aspects of the process in more detail. Finally, we bring our analysis down to the primary unit of socialisation within the school, namely, the classroom group itself. We discuss sociometric methods for analysing the classroom-group and outline a model for such analysis.

NOTES

1. Floud, J. 'Teaching in the Affluent Society' in *The World Yearbook of Education* 1963.

2. Blyth, W. A. L. *English Primary Education*, Vol. 1 (Routledge & Kegan Paul 1965).

3. Turner, R. 'Contest and Sponsored Mobility and the School System', *Amer. Soc. Rev.*, pages 855–67 (1960).

4. Etzioni (27), page 70.

5. Blyth (as note 2), Vol. 1, page 86.

6. Floud (as note 1).

7. Johnson (50), page 214.

8. Bernstein, B. 'Open Schools Open Society?', *New Society* (14th September 1967).

9. See Merton, R. K. 'The Role-set: Problems in Sociological Theory', *B.S.J.* (8) (1957).

10. See Hudson, L. *Contrary Imaginations* (Methuen 1968) and Warburton, F. W. 'Attainment and the School Environment' in Wiseman (109), chapter 6, Sears (139) and Vernon (143).

11. Floud, J. 'The Sociology of Education' in Welford (101).

12. Sapir, E. *Language* (Harcourt, Brace (USA) 1921).

13. Gross, Neal 'The Sociology of Education' in Merton (72), page 143.

14. Waller (99), page 195.

15. As adapted in Havighurst and Neugarten (44), page 512, from Thelen (94), pages 511–12.

16. There are a number of different sources in which this study and others similar can be examined, possibly the best is White, R. and Lippitt, R. *Autocracy and Democracy*: *An Experimental Enquiry* (Harper (USA) 1960).

17. Withall, J. and Lewis, W. W. 'Social Interaction in the Classroom' in Gage, N. G. (Ed.) *Handbook of Research on Teaching* (Rand McNally (USA) 1963).

18. Jennings (48), page 11.

19. Parsons, T. 'The School Class as a Social System' in Halsey (40).

20. Getzels, J. W. and Thelen, H. A. 'The Classroom as a Unique Social System' in *The Dynamics of Instructional Groups* – the 59th Yearbook of the National Society for the Study of Education, Part II. Henry, N. B. (Ed.) (University of Chicago Press (USA) 1960), page 53.

21. *Ibid.*, as adapted from figure on page 80.

22. *Ibid.*, page 73.

23. *Ibid.*, page 77.

24. *Ibid.*, page 77.

FURTHER READING

Volume I of Blyth (see note 2) includes a sociological description of the English primary school, and provides a useful outline of aspects of the educational system.

Lawton (55) reviews the research relating to the influence of social class and environment on language and pays specific attention to education.

Olmsted (82) consists of a short introduction to small group studies. This is a useful book for obtaining an outline of some of the problems and issues in this field.

See Bany and Johnson (5) for a summary of many of the small-group studies relating to education, together with examples and suggestions of how this can aid the teacher in the classroom. The whole book is relevant to the classroom-group situation.

Getzels and Thelen (see note 20) contains a collection of articles on classroom-group behaviour, including a model of the classroom.

Bibliography

Books

1. Abrams, M. *The Teenage Consumer* (London Press Exchange 1960)
2. Aron. R. *Main Currents in Sociological Thought*, Vol. 2 (Weidenfeld & Nicolson 1968)
3. Bales, R. F. *Interaction Process Analysis* (Addison Wesley 1950)
4. Banks, Olive *The Sociology of Education* (Batsford 1968)
5. Bany, Mary A. & Johnson, Lois *Group Dynamics in Education* (Macmillan 1964)
6. Bell, W. E. & Vogel, E. F. *A Modern Introduction to the Family* (Free Press (USA) 1960)
7. Biddle, B. J. & Thomas, E. J. *Role Theory, Concepts and Research* (Wiley (USA) 1966)
8. Bott, Elizabeth *The Family and Social Network* (Tavistock 1957)
9. Bottomore, T. B. *Sociology: A Guide to Problems and Literature* (Unwin University Books 1962)
10. Broom, L. & Selznick, P. *Sociology* (Harper & Row 1966)
11. Burgess, E. W. & Locke, H. J. *From Institution to Companionship* (American Book Co. (USA) 1953)
12. Carter, M. *Home, School and Work* (Pergamon Press 1962)
13. Cartwright, D. & Zander, A. *Group Dynamics* (Tavistock 1961)
14. Cooley, C. H. *Human Nature and the Social Order* (Schocken, Bailey Bros. 1964)
15. Corwin, R. G. *A Sociology of Education* (Appleton (USA) 1965)
16. Coser, L. *The Functions of Social Conflict* (Routledge & Kegan Paul 1956)
17. Cotgrove, S. *The Science of Society* (Allen & Unwin 1967)
18. Craft, M. *Linking Home and School* (Longmans 1967)
19. Davis, Kingsley *Human Society* (Macmillan 1949)
20. Douglas, J. W. B. *The Home and the School* (MacGibbon & Kee 1964)
21. Downes, D. M. *The Delinquent Solution* (Routledge & Kegan Paul 1962)

22. Durkheim, E. *Education and Sociology* (Free Press (USA) 1956)

23. Durkheim, E. *The Rules of Sociological Method* (Collier-Macmillan 1964)

24. Eisenstadt, S. N. *From Generation to Generation* (Routledge & Kegan Paul 1956)

25. Elkin, F. *Child and Society* (Random House (USA) 1960)

26. Erikson, E. H. (Ed.) *Youth: Change and Challenge* (Basic Books 1963)

27. Etzioni, A. *A Comparative Analysis of Complex Organisations* (Free Press (USA) 1961)

28. Etzioni, A. *Modern Organisations* (Prentice-Hall 1964)

29. Evans, K. M. *Sociometry and Education* (Routledge & Kegan Paul 1962)

30. Faris, R. E. L. (Ed.) *Handbook of Modern Sociology* (Rand McNally 1964)

31. Floud, J., Halsey, A. H. & Martin, F. M. *Social Class and Educational Opportunity* (Heinemann 1957)

32. Fraser, E. D. *Home and Environment and the School* (University of London Press 1959)

33. Glass, D. V. *Social Mobility in Great Britain* (Routledge & Kegan Paul 1954)

34. Gorer, G. *Exploring English Character* (Cresset Press 1955)

35. Gould, J. & Kolb, W. L. *A Dictionary of the Social Sciences* (Tavistock 1964)

36. Green, Bryan S. R. & Johns, E. A. *An Introduction to Sociology* (Pergamon Press 1967)

37. Gross, Neal, Mason, W. S. & McEarchen, A. W. *Explorations in Role Analysis: Studies of the School Superintendency Role* (Wiley 1958)

38. Hall, M. Penelope *The Social Services of Modern England* (Routledge 1964)

39. Halloran, J. D. *The Effects of Mass Communication with Special Reference to Television* (Leicester University Press 1965)

40. Halsey, A. H., Floud, J. & Anderson, C. *Education, Economy and Society* (Free Press (USA) 1961)

41. Hansen, D. A. & Gerstl, Joel E. *On Education: Sociological Perspectives* (Wiley 1967)

42. Hare, F. P. *Handbook of Small Group Research* (Free Press (USA) 1962)

43. Hare, F., Borgatta, E. F. & Bales, R. F. *Small Groups: Studies in Social Interaction* (Knop (USA) 1955)

44. Havighurst, R. F. & Neugarten, B. L. *Society and Education* (Allyn & Bacon 1962)

45. Hoggart, R. *The Uses of Literacy* (Penguin 1965)

46. Homans, G. *The Human Group* (Routledge & Kegan Paul 1951)

47. Jackson, B & Marsden, D. *Education and the Working Class* (Routledge & Kegan Paul 1962)

48. Jennings, Helen H. *Sociometry in Group Relations* (American Council of Education (USA) 1948)

49. Jennings, Hilda, *Societies in the Making* (Routledge & Kegan Paul 1962)

50. Johnson, H. M. *Sociology: A Systematic Introduction* (Routledge & Kegan Paul 1961)

51. Jones, Howard *Reluctant Rebels* (Tavistock 1960)

52. Kelsall, R. K. *Population* (Longmans 1967)

53. Klein, J. *Samples from English Cultures,* Vols I and II (Routledge & Kegan Paul 1965)

54. Kuper, Leo *Living in Towns* (Cresset Press 1953)

55. Lawton, D. *Social Class, Language and Education* (Routledge & Kegan Paul 1968)

56. Lazarsfeld, P. F. & Rosenberg, M. *Language of Social Research* (Free Press (USA) 1965)

57. Lewis, M. M. *Language, Thought and Personality* (Nottingham University Press 1963)

58. Loomis, C. P. & Loomis, Z. K. *Modern Social Theories* (Van Nostrand (U.S.A.) 1961)

59. MacIver, R. M. & Page, C. H. *Society: An Introductory Analysis* (Macmillan 1961)

60. McLelland, D. C. *Talent and Society* (Van Nostrand (USA) 1958)

61. McLelland, D. C. *et al. The Achievement Motive* (Appleton (USA) 1953)

62. McLelland, D. C. *The Achieving Society* (Free Press (USA) 1961)

63. Maccoby, E. E., Newcomb, T. M. & Hortley, E. L. *Readings in Social Psychology* (Methuen 1959)

64. Martindale, D. *The Nature and Types of Sociological Theory* (Routledge & Kegan Paul 1962)

65. Mays, J. B. *Education and the Urban Child* (Liverpool University Press 1962)

66. Mead, G. H. *Mind, Self and Society* Morris, C. W. (Ed.) (University of Chicago Press (USA) 1934)

67. Mead, Margaret *Cooperation and Competition* (Beacon Howe (USA) 1961)

68. Mead, Margaret *Growing up in New Guinea* (Penguin 1961)

69. Mead, Margaret *Male and Female* (Penguin 1964)

70. Mead, Margaret *Sex and Temperament* (Dell 1967)

71. Merton, Robert K. *Social Theory and Social Structure* (Free Press (USA) 1957)

72. Merton, Robert K. *et al Sociology Today: Problems and Prospects* (Basic Books 1959)

73. Mills, C. Wright *The Sociological Imagination* (Oxford University Press 1967)

74. Mitchell, G. Duncan *A Dictionary of Sociology* (Tavistock 1964)

75. Mogey, J. *Family and Neighbourhood* (Oxford University Press 1956)

76. Moreno, J. L. *Who Shall Survive?* (Beacon House (USA) 1953)

77. Murdock, G. P. *Social Structure* (Macmillan (USA) 1949)

78. Musgrave, P. W. *The Sociology of Education* (Methuen 1965)

79. Musgrave, P. W. *The School as an Organisation* (Macmillan 1968)

80. Musgrove, F. W. *Youth and the Social Order* (Routledge & Kegan Paul 1964)

81. Myrdal, A. & Klein, V. *Women's Two Roles* (Routledge & Kegan Paul 1962)

82. Olmsted, M. *The Small Group* (Random House (USA) 1959)

83. Parsons, Talcott *Societies: Evolutionary and Comparative Perspectives* (Prentice-Hall 1966)

84. Parsons, Talcott *The Social System* (Tavistock 1952)

85. Parsons, Talcott & Bales, R. F. *Family, Socialisation and Interaction Process* (Free Press (USA) 1955)

86. Parsons, Talcott & Shils, E. *Towards a General Theory of Action* (Harvard University Press (USA) 1951)

87. Piaget, Jean *The Moral Judgement of the Child* (Free Press (USA) 1948)

88. Rodman, H. *Marriage, Family and Society* (Random House (USA) 1965)

89. Rosser, C. & Harris, C. *The Family and Social Change* (Routledge & Kegan Paul 1965)

90. Sills, D. L. *The International Encyclopedia of Social Sciences* (Collier-Macmillan 1968)

91. Slater, E. & Woodside, M. *Patterns of Marriage* (Cassell 1951)

92. Spencer, H. *Education* (Cambridge University Press 1932)

93. Strauss, A. (Ed.) *The Social Psychology of George Herbert Mead* (Phoenix Books–University of Chicago Press 1959)

94. Thelen, H. A. *Dynamics of Groups at Work* (Phoenix (USA) 1954)

95. Thut, I. N. & Adams, D. K. *Educational Patterns in Comtemporary Societies* (McGraw-Hill 1964)

96. Timashaff, N. S. *Sociological Theory: Its Nature and Growth* (Random House (USA) 1955)

97. Townsend, P. *The Family Life of Old People* (Routledge & Kegan Paul 1957)

98. Veness, T. *School Leavers* (Methuen 1962)

99. Waller, Willard *The Sociology of Teaching* (Russell & Russell 1961)

100. Weber, Max *The Theory of Social and Economic Organisation* (Free Press (USA) 1947)

101. Welford, A. T. (Ed.) *et al Society* (Routledge & Kegan Paul 1962)

102. Williams, R. *Britain in the Sixties* (Penguin 1962)

103. Williams, R. *Communications* (Chatto & Windus 1966)

104. Willmott, Pauline *A Consumer Guide to the Social Services* (Penguin 1962)

105. Willmott, Pauline *The Evolution of a Community* (Routledge & Kegan Paul 1963)

106. Wilson, Everett K. *Sociology: Rules, Roles and Relationships* (Dorsey 1966)

107. Winch, Robert *The Modern Family* (Holt, Rinehart & Winston 1966)

108. Winch, Robert, McGinnis, R. & Barringer, H. R. (Eds.) *Selected Studies in Marriage and the Family* (Holt, Rinehart & Winston (USA) 1962)

109. Wiseman, Stephen *Education and the Environment* (Manchester University Press 1964)

110. Young, M. *Innovation and Research in Education* (Routledge & Kegan Paul 1965)

111. Young, M. & Willmott, P. *Family and Kinship in East London* (Routledge & Kegan Paul 1957)

112. Young, M. & Willmott, P. *Family and Class in a London Suburb* (Routledge & Kegan Paul 1960)

113. Zimmerman, Carle *Family and Civilisation* (Harper & Row (USA) 1947)

Articles

114. Ashley, B. J. 'Factors in Organisation: some social and environmental issues', *T.E.S.* (Scotland) (January 1967)

115. Ashley, B. J., Cohen, H. & Slatter, R. 'Social Classifications', *T.E.S.* (Scotland) (17th March 1967)

116. Ashley, B. J., Cohen, H. & Slatter, R. 'Why We are Teachers' *T.E.S.* (Scotland) (12th May 1967)

117. Becker, H. S. 'Social Class Variations in the Teacher–Pupil Relationship', *J. Educ. Soc.*, 27 (April 1952)

118. Bernstein, B. 'A Socio-Linguistic Approach to Social Learning', *Social Science Survey*, Gould, J. (Ed.) (Penguin 1965)

119. Bernstein, B. 'Language and Social Class', *Br. J. Soc.*, (2) (1960)

120. Bernstein, B. 'Social Structure, Language and Learning', *Educ. Research*, (3) (1961)

121. Blake, J. & Davis, K. 'Norms, Values and Sanctions' *Handbook of Sociology* in Faris (30).

122. Blyth, W. A. L. 'The Sociometric Study of Children's Groups in an English School', *Br. J. of Educ. Stud.* (May 1960)

123. Davis, K. 'The Myth of Functional Analysis As a Special Method in Sociology and Anthropology', *Amer. Soc. Rev.*, 24 (6) (December 1959)

124. Etzioni, A. 'Toward a Theory of Societal Guidance', *A.J.S.*, 73 (2) (1967)

125. Fallding, H. 'The Empirical Study of Values', *Amer. Soc. Rev.*, 30 (April 1965)

126. Holly, D. N. 'Profiting from a Comprehensive School', *Br. J. Soc.* (June 1965)

127. Hopper, E. I. 'Educational Systems', *Sociology*, (2) No. 1 (January 1968)

128. Kemp, L. C. D. 'Environmental and Other Characteristics Determining Attainment in Primary Schools', *Br. J. Educ. Psych.*, (25) (February 1955)

129. Kohn, M. L. 'Social Class and Parental Values', *Amer. J. Soc. Rev.*, (LXIV) (June 1959)

130. Kohn, M. L. 'Social Class and the Exercise of Parental Authority', *Amer. Soc. Rev.* (June 1959)

131. Lee, D. J. 'Class Differentials in Educational Opportunity', *Sociology*, (2) No. 3 (September 1968)

132. Lessnoff, M. H. 'Parsons' Systems Problems', *The Sociological Review*, (16) No. 2 (July 1968)

133. Little, Alan & Westergaard, John 'The Trend of Class Differentials in Educational Opportunity in England and Wales', *Br. J. of Soc.*, (XV) No. 4 (1964)

134. Litvack, E. 'Occupational Mobility and Extended Family Cohesion', *Amer. Soc. Rev.* (February 1960)

135. Marshall, T. F. & Mason, A. 'A Framework for the Analysis of Juvenile Delinquency Causation', *Br. J. Soc.*, (XIX) No. 2 (June 1968)

136. Mizruchi, E. & Perucci, R. 'Norm Qualities and Deviant Behaviour' *Amer. Soc. Rev.*, 27 (June 1962)

137. Musgrove, F. & Taylor, P. H. 'Teachers' and Parents' Conception of the Teacher's Role', *Br. J. Educ. Psych.*, 35 (2) (June 1965)

138. Ottaway, A. K. C. 'Durkheim on Education', *Br. J. Educ. Stud.*, 16 (1) (February 1968)

139. Sears, P. & Helgard, E. R. 'The Teacher's Role in the Motivation of the Learner', *63rd NSSE Yearbook* (University of Chicago Press 1964)

140. Stevens, E. 'Bibliographical Note: G. H. Mead', *Amer. J. Soc.*, 72 (5) (1967)

141. Swift, D. F. 'Educational Psychology, Sociology and the Environment', *Br. J. Soc.* (December 1965)

142. Swift, D. F. 'Social Class and Achievement Motivation', *Educ. Research,* (**VIII**) No. 2 (1966); 'Who Passes the 11 + ?', *New Society* (5th March 1964)

143. Vernon, P. E. 'Creativity and Intelligence', *Educ. Research*, 6 (1964)

144. Westwood, L. J. 'The Role of the Teacher II', *National Foundation for Educational Research*, No. 1 (**10**) (1967)

145. Wilson, B. R. 'The Teacher's Role', *Br. J. Soc.* (**13**) (1962)

146. Withall, J. 'The Development of a Climate Index', *J. Educ. Research*, 45 (1951)

147. Withall, J. 'The Development of a Technique for the Measurement of a Social-Educational Climate in Classrooms', *J. Exp. Educ.*, 17 (March 1949)

148. *Government reports* Published by HMSO.

Bruntlon *From School to Further Education* (1963)
Newsom *Half Our Future* (1963)
Robbins *Committee on Higher Education* (1963)
Plowden *Children and their Primary Schools*, Vols. 1 and 2 (1967)
Hadow *Report of Consultative Committee on the Primary School* (1931)
Norwood *Curriculum and Exams in Secondary Schools* (1943)
Spens *Report of Consultative Committee on Secondary Education* (1939)

Glossary

Note: Terms which are fully discussed in the text are not necessarily defined in the glossary.

ACHIEVEMENT. The situation where determinants of the individual's status and roles are, in the main, dependent upon his own capacity and performance.

AFFECTIVITY–AFFECT VEINEUTRALITY. A role may permit certain kinds of expression of feeling (affect) or may require that these kinds of expression be held in check. Thus, a familial role, such as that of mother, might be expected to be affective, but a professional role, such as that of child-care officer, might be expected to be affectively neutral.

ASCRIPTION. The situation where determinants of an individual's status and role are beyond his control, i.e. age, sex and caste.

BUREAUCRATIC. Most important sociological usage is that of Max Weber to depict a specific type of organisation based on a number of criteria among which are hierarchy of authority, documentation, rules of office and permanent salaried staff.

CHARISMATIC. (From Greek meaning 'divine grace'.) Used by Max Weber to describe a leader with special inner qualities such as religious prophets, or others whose following is based on their personality.

CULTURAL. 'Cultural in its broadest definition refers to that part of the total repertoire of human action (and its products), which is socially as opposed to genetically transmitted' (74, page 47).

DEFERRED GRATIFICATION. A concept which describes the capacity to defer gratification of short-term needs in order to permit, in the long term, gratification of needs which are considered to be superior or more beneficial.

DIFFERENTIATION. The process by which general functions are separated into more specific and specialised functions as a system develops.

DIFFUSENESS – SPECIFICITY. The occupant of a role may have strictly defined obligations to a person with whom he is in interaction (i.e. 'specific'), as for instance, a doctor in regard to a patient, or relatively wide and indefinite obligations (i.e. diffuse), as involved in the role of friend or relative.

DYSFUNCTIONS. These are actions which decrease or lessen the adaption or adjustment of the social system.

ENDS. Aspects of any interacting situation both in the present or future which are seen as goals.

ENDOGAMY. The practice of marrying within a defined group, such as a tribe or a social class.

EXOGAMY. The practice of marrying outside a definite group, such as a tribe or a social class.

EXPECTATIONS. That part of a person's behaviour which is taking account of the likely future actions of others (and himself).

EXPRESSIVE BEHAVIOUR. That aspect of behaviour within groups which is concerned with mediation, conciliation, emotional development and warm relationships.

EXTENDED FAMILY. The involvement of the nuclear family unit in a larger more composite family unit usually through a linking of the nuclear family with one or other of their families of origin.

FOLKWAYS. Standards or expected patterns of social action which, if broken, are punishable by less extreme forms of sanctions, such as gossip or ridicule, than is the case with mores. They are considered as being important but not vital to the maintenance of a society's welfare.

FORMAL GROUP. A group in which roles and norms governing the interaction between members are laid down explicitly and each person's role is quite clearly and explicitly determined for him.

FUNCTIONS. These are actions which, taken together, increase or improve the adaptation or adjustment of the social system both internally and externally.

GEMEINSCHAFT GESSELSCHAFT. Used by the German sociologist, F. Tonnies, in a specialised sense to depict two different types of social systems. Can be translated as 'community' for *gemeinschaft* and 'society' for *gesselschaft*. They are used as ideal types which serve to differentiate between two types of actions, those based on communal factors and those based on contractual associations.

GROUP DYNAMICS. The study of the structure and functioning of small groups with particular references to the processes of change taking place in the group.

HOMOGAMY. The practice of marrying within one's own social group, or among people like oneself.

IDEAL TYPE. A concept introduced into sociology by Max Weber, by which certain trends in observed phenomena are isolated and emphasised as generalised abstractions. The phenomena do not exist in the pure and extreme form, as described in an ideal type, which is used as an aid to analysis.

IDEOGRAPHIC. A term used by Getzels and Thelen to describe individuals, personality and need-dispositions, which together constitute what they call the personal and psychological dimension of their model of the classroom as a social system.

INFORMAL GROUP. A group in which the interaction between members is governed by the spontaneous emergence of roles and norms, and each person's role is determined during the course of spontaneous interaction.

IN GROUP. Any group which separates itself from other groups and considers itself distinct from these groups.

INSTITUTIONALISATION. The process whereby behaviour becomes regularised and associated with particular functions within a social system.

INSTITUTIONS. A well-established pattern of behaviour, centred round particular functions and developing a structure of its own within a social system.

INSTRUMENTAL BEHAVIOUR. That aspect of behaviour within groups which is concerned with management, task orientation or goal attainment behaviour.

ISOLATE. A person who neither makes any choices himself nor is chosen by any of the others responding to the sociometric questionnaire.

JOINT CONJUGAL ROLE. A term used, in particular by Elizabeth Bott, to describe the role relationships in a family in which there are no clearly differentiated responsibilities for either husband or wife, and where each can equally assume responsibility and concern for wide areas of behaviour within the family unit.

LATENT FUNCTION. These are functions which are neither intended nor recognised as such by the members of the system.

MANIFEST FUNCTIONS. These are functions which are intended and recognised by the participants in the system.

MEANS. Aspects of any interaction situation in a social system, which are seen as instruments which actors can utilise to attain their ends.

MORES (singular: MOS). Standards or expected patterns of social action which, if broken, are punishable by more extreme forms of sanctions, usually banishment or death, than is the case with folkways. Mores are considered as being both important and vital to the maintenance of a society's welfare.

NEGLECTEE. A person choosing other people in response to a sociometric questionnaire, but who themselves remain unchosen.

NOMOTHETIC. A term used by Getzel and Thelen to describe institutions, roles and expectations which together constitute what they call the normative dimension in their model of the classroom system.

NORMS. A socially accepted standard of behaviour, thus a role, standard or expected pattern of social action.

NUCLEAR FAMILY. A small group composed of husband and wife and immature children and constituting a unit separate from the rest of the community. It is an autonomous unit, based on close emotional relationships between husband and wife and between parents and children.

OUT GROUP. All the groups other than the one which is being considered by the members as an in group.

POLYGAMY. The practice of marriage between one member of one sex and two or more members of the opposite sex.

PRIMARY GROUPS. Usually a small social group which is characterised by intimacy, a high degree of continous face-to-face association and which is relatively permanent.

QUALITY – PERFORMANCE. An incumbent's behaviour in a role might be analysed according to the 'qualities' which are particularly associated with him (e.g. age, sex, personality) or according to the performance which he achieves independently of his personal qualities.

REFERENCE GROUP. A group or category of people with which an individual compares himself, which provides him with a set of self-evaluations and a comparative form of reference.

REJECTEE. A person who is rejected by other people in response to a sociometric questionnaire.

RELATIVE DEPRIVATION. A term for describing the process whereby persons see themselves as being deprived by comparing themselves to others. This can be a favourable comparison, in which case we speak of relative gratification.

ROLE. A set of expectations applied to an incumbent in a particular position in a social setting.

ROLE CONFLICT. When a person finds that the performance of one role conflicts with his performance of another.

ROLE PERFORMANCE. The actual behavior of an actor while in a particular role.

ROLE SET. The complement or network of role relationships which persons have by virtue of occupying a particular position in a social system.

SECONDARY GROUP. Usually a large social group which is characterised by a lack of intimacy, a low degree of face-to-face association and is of relatively short duration compared to a primary group.

SECULARISATION. A term used to describe a process in which it is suggested that the secular values of society are becoming increasingly important as compared with the sacred or religious.

SEGREGATED CONJUGAL ROLE. A term used, in particular by Elizabeth Bott, to describe role relationships in a family in which husband and wife have specific and differentiated areas of responsibility and concern within the family unit.

SOCIAL ACTION. Behaviour which is intended to influence the actions of others, thus oriented towards other actors; action is non-social when oriented solely to inanimate objects.

SOCIAL CLASS. A complicated concept used by sociologists in a number of different ways. The most famous usage is that of Marx, where it is seen as a category of people who stand in the same relationship to the ownership of the means of production.

SOCIAL GROUP. Two or more persons who take each other into account in their actions and are, as a result, held together and set apart from others.

SOCIAL INTERACTION. The mutual and reciprocal influencing of each other's expectations of behaviour and actual behaviour by two or more people.

SOCIALISATION. The process by which the individual develops into a more or less adequate member of a social group. In this process, individuals acquire the already existing culture of the social groups they came into. 'Socialisation is learning to perform social roles' (50).

SOCIAL POSITION. The location of a person relative to other persons in a social system.

SOCIAL STRATIFICATION. This is a term used by the sociologist to refer to a particular kind of social differentiation, which includes the conception of a hierarchical ranking within the social system. Within this ranking, individuals may be placed and recognised as superior or inferior to other individuals who are differentiated from them according to some agreed criteria.

SOCIAL STRUCTURE. May be seen either as a network of social relationships among the members of a society, or as the organisation of the various institutions in the society.

SOCIAL SYSTEM. Consists of a plurality of individual actors, who are interacting with each other in a bounded situation in which they share common standards and values. The principle units of the social system and collectivities and roles. (Up to this point, the definition is Parsonian, but if we include the possibility of sub-systems emerging, which may not share the common standards and values of the total system, we allow at least some possibility of conflict.)

SOCIOMETRY. A theory and technique which has been developed for the study of interpersonal relations in groups. Particularly useful for representing graphically the patterns of attraction and repulsion among group members.

STAR. A person receiving a high number of choices in a sociometric questionnaire.

STATUS. The amount of power, prestige and wealth associated with a particular position in a social system.

UNIVERSALISM – PARTICULARISM. Obligations or responsibilities may be derived from a particular position, or may be derived from general criteria or values which have no attachment to a particular position, but depend on wide criteria universally exphasised with the social system.

VALUES. Are generalised common categories underlining a number of different norms. Thus, the social values of cleanliness is made 'specific' and 'effective' through numerous different norms.

Index

STONEHOUSE — NICE PLACE

NR. STROUD

1 FURTHER ON